CELEBRATING HOME

CELEBRATING HOME

A TIME FOR EVERY SEASON

JAMES T. FARMER III

Photographs by
EMILY FOLLOWILL

Foreword by
FURLOW GATEWOOD

GIBBS SMITH
TO ENRICH AND INSPIRE HUMANKIND

TO THE MEMORY OF MY BELOVED SAMPSON.

Through the love of our pets, our gardens and homes,
we come to love one another in thought and deed through each and every season.
"All creatures great and small," to borrow a phrase from James Herriot,
are creations of our God and King. It is the celebration of creation that allows
our hearts, minds and voices to sing. Alleluia!

Contents

FOREWORD, BY FURLOW GATEWOOD ... *7*

INTRODUCTION ... *9*

WINTER GATHERINGS ... *15*

CAMELLIA CELEBRATION ... *37*

FEAST AMONG THE FOXGLOVES ... *61*

BIRTHDAY DINNER IN CASHIERS ... *81*

SUMMER CALADIUM GARDEN ... *103*

SEPTEMBER CHARM ... *125*

DAHLIA DINNER ... *143*

ALFRESCO FALL ... *167*

FRIENDSGIVING IN CASHIERS ... *185*

THANKSGIVING ... *203*

COMFORT & JOY ... *231*

ACKNOWLEDGMENTS ... *270*

Foreword

I first met James Farmer in the fall of 2014. Our paths crossed as a result of the publishing of *One Man's Folly*; he contacted me about visiting and we arranged a date.

James is from Perry, Georgia, about an hour away from my homestead. Upon meeting, I quickly realized he was a fellow spirit. Besides the fact that we were both born and raised in small Georgia towns, we also shared interests in interior design, historic preservation, antiques, cooking, entertaining, and gardening, not to mention our profound love of animals.

James has a natural grace and outgoing personality. These features, along with his love of family and dedication to friends, is commendable and quite apparent when spending time with him. To James, home is much more than just a place. It is the setting of hospitality, where the act of providing kindnesses to one another happens. Making all invited feel like part of the family is second nature to James. Good food, good drink, shared conversation in a beautiful setting—it all comes together, resulting in what can only be described as Southern Style.

Having recently turned 100, I draw great pride in seeing the next generation of a Southern Gentleman. James is every part of this cohort. Excelling in generosity of spirit, he respects tradition while embracing new experiences, giving a fresh voice to his generation.

—FURLOW GATEWOOD

Introduction

"What I love about the South is that there is nothing
too insignificant to celebrate, and if you're really lucky you learn about
grace and small joys, which are, after all, what make up big lives."

—JULIA REED

"Nothing too insignificant to celebrate . . ." Perhaps that is why I love a dinner party—impromptu or planned, in the garden, on the porch or in the dining room, seasonally inspired or sentimentally set. We Southerners celebrate home and the delights therein with style, grace and juxtaposition—that calling card of mixing our heirloom silver and fried chicken, yard flowers and porcelain, garden vegetables and fine china—denoting our hallmark of hospitality.

My grandmother, Mimi, always said that "we eat with our eyes first." Before the first bite, there is a visual feast. We see the flowers and place settings. We behold the details of the table, exclaim, "This looks delicious," and continue to visually take it all in, before tasting anything. And then we eagerly plate our food, continuing to absorb the experience.

Much like interior design, assembling a dinner party engages all the elements of décor. For an interiors project, lead times take precedence over the creative process. The waiting and expectation, the delays and time crunches, the backorders and discontinued items are hurdles to navigate all along the way. Yet, when I'm setting a table, hosting a dinner party and cooking a meal, all these macro elements of design become a microcosm set within the confines of my porch, dining room or garden. A tablescape is simply that: a table set with all the trimmings one's creative prowess can conjure, an interior design project in its simplest form. And, bonus—there is usually no heavy furniture to move, walls to paint or impatient waiting for that hand-blocked linen from Europe. Creating a tablescape, for me, scratches an itch to design, with near-instant gratification.

Those with a creative bent, knack and sway—myself included—thrive when assembling found items and collected treasures. We love to interweave food and flowers, mixing our plates and patterns, trying different linens, being inspired by the season, a blossom or a new recipe. The seasons set my palette. The swan song of the blooming foxgloves is reason enough to host a dinner party. When the camellias are blooming, January through March, I truly need a time to celebrate these roses of winter that inspire and rejuvenate me during the gravest of cold weeks.

Introduction

True luxury for me is staying home because my work as an author and interior designer—though both are my dream jobs—involves travel and physical toil and requires a wellspring of energy. So, when the opportunity presents itself to be "set put," as a dear friend used to say, I seize the chance and relish the moments when I am home. Using my dinnerware, polishing my silver, cooking favorite dishes and clipping flowers from my beloved garden to adorn my table is what I love! Whether home in Georgia at Farmdale or in the mountains of North Carolina at Joe Pye Cottage, hosting a gathering of friends and family reminds me of another quote from Mimi: "We feed people—body and soul—at our tables."

I can wholeheartedly say that this bodes true for me as a host. I am fed by the exercise of creativity that entertaining evokes and the hope that my guests leave my table with more than a meal, perhaps some spiritual sustenance and inspiration to share with those they encounter. It is from the garden, nature and the seasons that I take my inspiration, borrowing the colors, hues, textures and tones of the time and recreating them in a tableau—a feast for the senses with the added bonus of soulful nourishment.

Introduction

I channel my grandmother when I entertain and try my best to embody her graciousness and warmth. My mother's humor and love of beauty come through as I'm setting the table and fondly remembering her stories. One of my very first memories is the smell of a tomato being picked: I'm in Granddaddy's arm while the tomato is plucked from the vine with his other. That scent takes me to his garden, as does the sight of fluffy mophead hydrangeas mounded in a hedge or centerpiece. We entertain to celebrate. We entertain to cherish life and legacy. We entertain to open our hearts and homes to those we love. This is the mantle given to me by my family. There is nothing too insignificant to celebrate.

Allow me to take you on a tour of my homes and gardens, set a place for you at my table and inspire you to do the same for those you love. The seasons bring us a gracious plenty to offer our friends and family. They denote mile markers in our lives that can be simultaneously sweet and bittersweet. This complexity of emotions falls into that cadre of Southern style in the way we contrast the old and the new, the found and forgotten with the fine and the everyday. And this stamp of Southern style is reinforced with each season, with each camellia in a silver punch bowl, recipe recreated and revived, or dahlia donning a harvest celebration table.

From winter to spring, we long for the warmth and verdant seasons to come, recalling the holidays and harvest beforehand. Indoors, I love to mimic the crispness of winter's palette with whites and blues, branches and boughs, and that touch of sparkle the icy months can bring. As we begin to thaw, a celebration of familial birthdays coincides with the height of camellia season. Here is my excuse to use the silver and crystal that represent recent generations and toast their legacies. The garden begins to wake from a winter's nap as nothing short of horticultural magic turns the world green again, as my foxgloves—planted two seasons prior—bolt and bloom! I find myself outside again, hands in the dirt; spring is healing and gardening is cathartic for me. Light suppers outdoors with bouquets of roses and bottles of rosé create the most delightful of spring evenings.

The heat is on the horizon, which means my garden will be brimming with caladiums all summer long. Then late dinners in the golden hours of evening have us lingering longer around the table. The mountains begin their call this season too, and the altitude lifts my attitude once the summer heat drives us up the winding roads to seek solace in the cooler air. My porch becomes my dining room and the serenade of nature's choir revives our wilted spirits.

There's a magical time between seasons in the mountains, when peaches and pumpkins collide at the farmers market, apples begin to taunt us with their nostalgic flavors, and the tinge of autumnal change is looming. The end of summer melting into fall is spectacular in the highlands of Western North Carolina. Dahlias, hydrangeas, asters, and anemones create a floral crescendo in the garden before the fall foliage becomes the main attraction.

Introduction

Once the leaves turn their brilliant kaleidoscope of colors, warm days yield to cool nights, when alfresco suppers are still truly lovely but the lure of the table indoors and the approaching holidays begins to beckon. Cornucopias of flavors and colors create tablescapes laden with the last of the dahlias and feasts of flavors reflecting the season. Thanksgiving—the holiday proper and the very feeling—comes to mind and fruition. Time and tradition bring us to another holiday season, and Christmas, we know, is not far.

As we are home for Christmas, the seasons wind down, but not without a burst of all the layers this holiday bestows. The food and flowers challenge me each year to embrace the traditions yet give them a twist of my own design. Mimi's punch bowl may have served us eggnog in the past, but the vessel also looks quite stunning holding amaryllis and magnolia. Mama's Christmas china, which she purchased in an antique shop and then went into labor with me (can't make that up!), is once again at our table, serving a favorite cake and cups of coffee after a Christmas dinner.

As the holidays fade into a memory and new chapters have been written as seasonal entries in the stories of our lives, the cycle, circle and concentricity of life begins again with a new year. I find myself ebbing and flowing, waxing and waning with each year. However, the constant, for me, is the ever-present reverence of the season. The source of inspiration for each dinner party's theme, flavor and décor.

Each season is a salute to nature's bounty, a family's heritage and the undercurrent of love we share. As for me and my house, commemorating each milestone or minute with that love is a true delight. Whether a birthday, holiday or significantly insignificant day, may we always long to be at home, honoring the times we share there, treasuring the traditions and generations represented therein, and rediscovering the joy our homes and gardens bring to our lives.

Join me on this journey in *Celebrating Home*. May your home be blessed with the marks of every passing season as true observances of the grace-filled small joys that truly make our lives big.

PLEASE JOIN ME FOR

A Wintertime Dinner

January 28

Joe Pye Cottage

six o'clock until

Répondez s'il vous plaît

THOUGH IT MAY BE COLD YET BRIGHT
IT WOULD BRING ME SUCH DELIGHT
FOR YOU TO JOIN ME
ON THIS WINTER'S NIGHT

THE FIRE WILL BRING US WARMTH AND CHEER
AND FILL OUR HEARTS THIS TIME OF YEAR
TO BE GATHERED WITH ONES SO DEAR

Winter Gatherings

Winter Gatherings

Not long after the glow of the holidays has waned, we find ourselves amidst a wintry landscape void of the verdant foliage of seasons past. Bare branches replace flowery beds, and the gray sky can be mimicked on the ground. In this time of cold, our spirits and the weather can feel one and the same. However, gathering friends and family for the sole reason of being together is a celebration.

In this season, we crave that particular warmth the fellowship around our tables can provide—not only sustenance as a meal but that soulful nourishment we often need during our "winters." As the temperatures fall outdoors, I turn my attention to creating warmth indoors.

A winter dinner party provides a moment to look for the beauty of the season rather than focus on the lack thereof. The structure of tree branches, the audacious hope of early blooming bulbs, and the persistence of evergreens inspire celebratory tablescapes and tableaus. Keeping a crisp palette of whites, greens, and soft blues, my tables and place settings are reminiscent of the snowy mountainside in Cashiers. Spending time at Joe Pye Cottage during the winter gives me the taste of the season that I do not experience in South Central Georgia.

Budded quince branches, paperwhites, amaryllis, tulips, and hyacinth serve as forced bulbs and cut stems for the tabletop and bar. Evergreen Ligustrum, with its deep purple berries, sets off ranunculus, roses, and anemones in centerpieces along with collars of Galax—a perennial evergreen and hopeful reminder of the lush summer season to come in the mountains.

One of my favorite plants and flowers is the Lenten rose. These hellebores are harbingers of hope, not only symbolically but horticulturally; they emerge in the coldest time and even dare to flower! I love to use them as a potted composition and plant them outside in the garden after the dinner party.

For the place settings, I often use pottery pieces. These soft blue and creamy white plates by Mollie Jenkins, my vintage brass bamboo flatware, and chargers by Provvista Designs create the tableau. Clear glassware, hurricanes, and vases shimmer in the winter light and create a complementary juxtaposition to the earthenware. Bright green apples and pears are a nod to the dessert and keep my mantra of "eating with our eyes first" in play.

Winter Gatherings

As for the main menu, bright greens in the salad and fruit platter not only provide important vitamins for the wintertime but nourish us visually as well. I like to serve the Southern classic Country Captain during winter, as its warm colors, textures, and flavors offset the chilly temperatures outside. A twist on a curry chicken dish, Country Captain is made all the better by accompaniments of chutney, dried fruit, and nuts. For added health benefit and visual delight, a pavlova topped with an apple and pear conserve, blackberries, and pomegranate arils round out the dinner. A warm mug of coffee with Irish cream ensures a merry end to a gratifying meal.

All-in-all, there is beauty to be found in every season. Winter's elegance inspires dinners like these, which keep our minds, bodies, and spirits warm. I am thankful for every opportunity to host friends and family around my table. May we continually seek beauty in life—even in the coldest months. It is the communion of friends that can thaw our most wintry seasons.

PRECEDING OVERLEAF: My dear friend Libby Endry, of the Gardner's Cottage in Asheville, helped me plan this dinner. Her use of wintry white flowers and elegant evergreens set the scene.

OPPOSITE: Often in the mountains, bluebird days give us a bright and clear sky in the midst of the winter season. This was the inspiration for the tablecloth; as seen in nature, blue offsets the evergreens and white clouds or snow, as this cloth does with the white flowers.

Winter Gatherings

OPPOSITE: Though often used on spring tables, bulbous flowers such as tulips, hyacinths, amaryllis, and paperwhites can be forced and thus used as planted compositions or as cut stems gathered in crisp, elegant winter bouquets.

ABOVE: A potted composition can be just as stellar as cut flowers in a vase. These hellebores are perennial plants and will subsequently be planted outside to bloom again in late winters to come.

Winter Gatherings

OPPOSITE: Paperwhites and other narcissus make great cut flowers, but I keep them arranged together, as their sap can shorten the lifespan of other cut flowers. Twigs and tulips in Vicky Miller pottery look as if they were taken from the painting behind. I love when tulips begin to open up. Pine cones and lichens fill another pottery piece.

ABOVE: I love to set a bar in the living room at Joe Pye. Guests can help themselves, and it's a great way to start and conclude a dinner party. The wintry woods beyond inspired this vignette.

OVERLEAF: Silver, brass and crystal, cut glass and heart pine—the melding and mixing of textures create similar tones too. White pottery and a favorite tureen hold amaryllis, Ligustrum and pears. Green parrot tulips are hopeful reminders of spring.

Winter Gatherings

PRECEDING OVERLEAF: I like to combine glass, silver and brass for what I call a winter shimmer. The mix of metals and glass reminds me of snowflakes and icicles set against the mountain landscape. With a serene, clean table setting of predominantly green and white, I like for the menu's palette to bring some warmth to the tablescape.

OPPOSITE: An after-dinner fire is the perfect perch for catching up with friends and toasting those friendships. Yellow is such a harbinger of hope, to me. Early, forced daffodils in a simple pottery jug note the coming season.

ABOVE: Crisp, bright greens and lemony dressing ward away wintertime blues. Celery leaves add great flavor and texture to salads.

Winter Gatherings

Winter Gatherings

PRECEDING OVERLEAF: I love to serve Country Captain during the winter, specifically for the sides that garnish it. Chicken thighs are hearty and a great foundation for chutney, dried fruit and nuts. A favorite recipe inspiration is from *Charleston Receipts*, first published by the Junior League of Charleston in 1950.

OPPOSITE: I crave fruit in the winter. A platter of vitamins and color is the perfect complement to a hearty supper. It's a great side for any meal or snack during the season. Wedges of pineapple with their tufts add flair.

ABOVE: Pavlova reminds me of snow on the mountain peaks. Brightness from pomegranate arils and blackberries is complemented by an applesauce spiced with cinnamon, ginger and cardamom. Easiest recipe: cook down peeled apples, then sweeten and season to taste with your favorite spices—delicious!

You're Invited To
A Camellia Celebration

A Luncheon at Farmdale
February 24, 2021
Noon until Spring

Winter has Settled, yet Spring's Warmth is Near
Camellia's Beauty Brings Joy Each Year
In Shades of Pink, White, and Red
We celebrate—
For Spring is Ahead

Camellia Celebration

Camellia Celebration

The month of February is monumental in scope for my family. Though the shortest month of the year, it holds weighty anniversaries, birthdays and celebratory joy—all combined in a few short weeks. My sister, Meredith, and I celebrate our kidney transplant anniversary early in the month, which is an exceptional event to celebrate. However, the date coincides with our mother's passing—making the time bittersweet.

As the month progresses, the anniversary of losing our beloved grandfather approaches, and I recall using gorgeous pink camellias from his yard at his service. The end of the month is capped with a triumvirate of birthdays noteworthy and quite remarkable: my great-grandmother, grandmother and mother all shared the same birthday!

I often jest about February being the shortest month but packing the biggest punch. As the emotions are taken for a roller coaster ride, my mind has to focus on the blessings that still abound—the legacies set into place in my life that have instilled in me a time to celebrate. To gather, feed, and toast the lives that gave me my heritage and roots, and to remember the love they gave me is comforting and gratifying. Choosing to celebrate can be a difficult decision at times, but I assure you, it's a choice that always dulls the sharpest grief with joy, fondness and warmth.

I remember how those three women who share that February birthday would often entertain for themselves—planning luncheons for one another with friends of all generations. I loved coming home from school and seeing ladies of all ages still lingering at the table or having coffee or tea late into the afternoon. I also recall the camellias—bowls and bowls of camellias floating down the table.

In my neck of the woods, where the winter climate is milder, camellias are at their crescendo this time of year and continue blooming well into late March. But in February, the camellias of my childhood memories continue to blossom and serve as links to those memorable February celebrations. As Southerners, any blossom, fruit or season is a reason to celebrate, and elegantly simple affairs are my favorites.

"Camellias arrange themselves," my great-grandmother told me. She would snip huge, deep magenta blooms with bright yellow stamens out of her yard and float them in glass, silver or crystal bowls around her house or as a centerpiece on her table. Those wise words are still my mantra today. I love to use Charleston camellia bowls for displaying the luscious blossoms. They're flared and shallow enough to display the flowers and do all the work for you. Camellias simply arrange themselves!

Camellia Celebration

Beyond the camellia bowls, I love to truly celebrate the lives and legacies of these three ladies with Southern savoir faire—pulling out familial pieces of silver, collecting pieces from dear friends and assembling them all on my dining table as an homage to my family, the season and the legacy of love bestowed upon me. I can just hear them saying, "Use your silver! You don't have to polish it as often if you're using it!"

A dear friend of mine, Jane Anne Sullivan, is gracious and generous beyond measure. She too shares my affinity for camellias and their symbolism and that homey tug on the heartstrings. Mixing some of her silver pieces with mine, we created a tablescape worthy of three birthdays, complete with a favorite menu these ladies loved (as does this gent!).

I have custom tablecloths made to suit my oblong tables. The base for this occasion is my camellia tablecloth, which boasts recognizable specimens of camellias and Southern foliage against a tea-colored ground. A silver epergne is layered with camellias in reds, pinks, fuchsia and variegated specimens. I often create a centerpiece with "satellites orbiting" around it on my table, creating varying heights, textures and tones on the tablescape.

Two Charleston camellia bowls flank the epergne centerpiece, brimming with variegated red, white and magenta blossoms, while silver baskets bobble with their bevy of 'Coral Delight' and 'Pink Perfection' camellias around the other arrangements. Citrus season coincides with camellia season in the Deep South, and the pairing of these two is quintessential and nostalgic—also alluding to a dessert to come! In the same family as camellias, tea olive is also blooming in late winter in the Southern landscape, and I love to use snips and clips of the fragrant flowers as an accent. A bouquet of tea olive in a silver container is simply chic and classic!

Southerners have long held an affinity for chinoiserie, and the pieces seen around my dining room are enhanced by reproduction Imari dinnerware mixes on the table and ceramic pagoda tulipieres of fluffy, ruffled, hot pink camellias. Pink cabbage plates serve as chargers for the luncheon place settings, since mixing styles and patterns creates cadence and visual appeal, especially when setting a table.

PRECEDING OVERLEAF: All set and ready to celebrate! My dining room at Farmdale faces south, and with wonderful light brick floors and large windows, it always feels like a conservatory or sunporch—perfect for a luncheon.

OPPOSITE: My friend and most talented floral designer Mary Pinson crafted the wreaths from local camellia specimens in nearby Macon, thus adding a touch of whimsy to the elegant scene.

Camellia Celebration

Branches of redbud and 'Pink Perfection' camellias in vases adorn the mantel. Pink camellias symbolize a longing for someone and often represent someone who is missed—a special nod to the generations celebrated at this event. Bowls of citrus and camellias add their notes of the season to the coffee table, and a bouquet of white camellias in the stairwell embodies adoration.

A favorite acanthus leaf–motif pottery piece bursts forth with camellias and bamboo shoots, serving as a sentry between the living and dining rooms and linking the two with the common theme of the event. I love the contrast of the white, earthy glaze and the pink hues of the flowers against the patina of antique wood and the textured grass cloth reflected in the mirror behind.

After a meal of tea sandwiches, shrimp salad, carrot cake and lemon meringue pie, the lunch lingered into the afternoon, as my mother and grandmother would have loved, and a fire kept the festive afternoon warm.

I relish any opportunity to celebrate. The devotion shown at a memorial event is a continuation of the respect, love and honor I hold for the generations being honored. Using my familial and found objects, mixing them with dear friends' treasures and creating a festive tableau amidst a bittersweet time is truly heartwarming. I have found that "keeping the feast" after "communion" is the best therapy, healing and medicine for the soul.

In every time of year, nature provides a bounty. Taking inspiration from the season, the flowers and foliage speak to our eyes and hearts. Celebrating at home the lives of our family is a tradition I was taught and hope to instill for generations to come.

PRECEDING OVERLEAF: 'Coral Delight' is a favorite camellia cultivar of mine. Silver baskets filled with them and citrus are truly Southern icons of the season. The tablecloth is made of the "Elise" pattern by Carleton V and depicts camellias and nandina foliage in lovely hues. I first saw the fabric at Yeamons Hall in Charleston, years ago, and love to use it in my designs.

OPPOSITE: 'Pink Perfection', 'Frank Houser' and old-fashioned variegated cultivars of camellias fill silver pieces atop my table. My dear friend Jane Anne Sullivan loves camellia as well and lent me her epergne for the centerpiece. Her mother, Glo, also loved and grew camellias, and we continue our mothers' legacies together when we entertain and celebrate.

Needs permission

PRECEDING OVERLEAF: Mama loved peaches and pinks, greens and aquas, and I used these tones for the table settings. Aunt Irene's silver luncheon set is used (she was Mimi's paternal aunt and I have many fond memories of her). Cabbage leaf chargers, Gump's Imari-inspired china and monogrammed linens from Shuler Studio—something each of mine, Mama's and Mimi's atop the table.

OPPOSITE: Branches of redbud—one of the first buds to pop in our Southern landscape—flank two vases of 'Pink Perfection' camellias in antique jade-hued, glazed Chinese vases on the mantel.

ABOVE: Tea olives bloom in the late wintertime in the Deep South, and they are cousins to the camellia. Their scent is simply divine. Arranging camellias is easy: float them in a dish or bowl and they do the work for you.

Needs permission

PRECEDING OVERLEAF: Peach-toned, glazed bud vases dot the shelves of my Welsh cupboard, boasting buds of camellias. The first of the season's geraniums are nestled near the sunny window, awaiting their time in the garden. Spring is surely on the way!

ABOVE: White camellias are probably my favorite, but it is truly difficult to pick just one! They represent adoration, purity and good luck and often represent mother and child—apropos for this celebration!

OPPOSITE: Bamboo shoots and a myriad of camellias spring forth from an acanthus-leaf footed bowl. They bring the luncheon's festive feel into the living room. My favorite lamp—made from an Italian guinea figure—is proof of my adage that no good lamp started life as a lamp.

OVERLEAF: On my pair of Chinese demilunes in the dining room, branches of 'Okame' cherry fill the large hurricanes. Loquat foliage and more camellias round out the arrangements. The bar is set on one of the demilunes. A citrus-infused tea and a rosé are served with a salad luncheon. The lamps are made from midcentury Italian ceramic fruit compotes and continue my adage about good lamps.

Camellia Celebration

I inherited my love of tea sandwiches, shrimp salad, lemon meringue pie and carrot cake from Mama and Mimi. In recognition of their February birthdays, I used my grandmother's wedding china depicting violets to serve the cake, since late winter is the bloom time for violets in the South. After the meal, the lunch lingered into the afternoon, as my mother and grandmother would have loved, and a fire kept the festive afternoon warm.

YOU'RE INVITED TO WELCOME SPRINGTIME

AMONG THE FOXGLOVES AT FARMDALE

Cocktails in the Garden

SIX O'CLOCK IN THE EVENING

APRIL 28, 2021

The garden has awakened and
winter has been shaken
Foxgloves are blooming
and a feast we'll be consuming

Feast among the Foxgloves

Feast among the Foxgloves

For a splendid spring, plant in the fall. For a fabulous fall, plant in the spring. This has been a long-time gardening motto for me. In these days of instant gratification, there's something quite nostalgic and even enchanting about the cycle of seasons—a time to plant, a time to harvest and the anticipation of it all.

As an avid gardener, I'm reminded of the cadence of nature when planning ahead for planting seasons, that wonder and anticipation filling my soul subsequent to the physical act of planting and working. In my garden at Farmdale, I have learned the power of and the practice in patience with planting a season crop.

Each fall, I plant foxgloves in the parterres, and I know that these small plants I'm planting in November will overwinter and then bolt and bloom in April, in shades of peach and white. The five months of waiting and watching their dormancy never cease to amaze me, for when that dormancy is broken, the miracle of spring's healing commences upon the wintertime turmoil.

I find myself still in awe and wonder that these plants survive the cold and then bloom in fountains of bell-shaped blossoms come springtime. Plants are so brave. They thrive and survive through whatever the seasons bring them, and this is perhaps one of my earliest observations as a child and a reflection today—their remarkable resilience is truly inspirational! As their seasonal height is at its peak, I place myself in this orchestra of flowers any chance I can—including taking my morning coffee and entertaining with the foxgloves as a backdrop.

Springtime and summer alfresco entertaining and dining become the routine for these seasons, and I find my menus are much simpler as well. Fruit platters and cheese trays paired with great wines can be just the perfect way to start a meal in the garden—or even served as the menu items at sunset cocktail hour. I also love a progressive dinner too, where appetizers and drinks may be served in one place, dinner at the table and the dessert in the garden. This is living at its best to me, when the season and weather serve the main course—such as a foxglove garden in full flower—and everything else is simply a welcome addition.

Engaging all the senses in a garden is key to a wonderful experience, and adding the element of taste (or toasting for that matter) is delightful. Strawberry season coincides when the foxgloves bloom, so I relish the opportunity to serve dishes inspired by these sweet berries. Having dessert in the garden is one of my absolute favorite pastimes! Soaking up the last rays of a perfect spring day and embracing the longer daylight and golden hour's magical light defines the full experience of entertaining at, in and around your home.

Feast among the Foxgloves

In late April and early May, when the foxgloves are having their heyday in the garden, the first flush of garden roses is also putting on quite the show. I love to arrange bouquets of these gorgeous blooms as centerpieces on serving and dining tables in the garden. These roses, grown by sweet friend Mary Royal, are spectacular and fragrant—truly what my imagination would invent if I were to create a rose.

Arranged in various shades of salmon, coral, peach and soft pinks, these petals are reminiscent of the foxgloves' color scheme. I like to use varying shades of a color all within an arrangement. Here these roses in lovely shades of a spring sunset, casually arranged in an heirloom pitcher of similar tone, uplift the alfresco tablescape. Similarly, I will often take another shade closely related to the centerpiece and recreate the same effect. Creamy yellow, ochre and soft buttery yellow roses in a shorter ensemble help to create a table setting with cadence and visual appeal.

Springtime in my garden is more colorful than summertime. Once the heat sets in, I adhere to a "green and white is always right" color palette. The visual coolness of the green and white combo is needed for the hotter months. However, springtime is my time for a more colorful showing. The peach foxgloves are accented with hot coral geraniums dotted around the garden in mossy terra-cotta pots. In the steeple bed, which is the center point of the parterre garden, the green and white color scheme is reinforced amid the colorful flowers elsewhere.

White foxgloves, silvery green lamb's ear, chartreuse euphorbia and thick-leaved sedums grow together around the steeple, which came from an old church in nearby Macon. A few white geraniums repeat the foxgloves in the background. This cross axis of the garden is a visual rest amid all the color. The crispness of the green and white palette is complemented by the juxtaposition of the metal and rusted patina of the steeple, which adds vertical and architectural interest to the garden.

All in all, we Southerners must take advantage of springtime, as it is a fleeting season. Wedged between the milder, wet winter and the hot, humid summer, spring is a lovely time in the garden. Taking the party, dinner or just your morning coffee into the garden is a must. Celebrating the culmination of a flower's crowning achievement, a dinner, a dessert, or simply a glass of wine with friends in the garden is refreshing and so enjoyable. After all, months of planning, planting and anticipation went into this event.

PRECEDING OVERLEAF: Looking eastward as the sun rises, the parterre garden is awash in soft morning light. The centerpiece of the garden is a steeple from an old church in Macon, Georgia. I happened upon it one day and love the juxtaposition of its rusty patina with the brick and greenery.

OPPOSITE: I love seeing the morning light through the leaves of the loquat trees, which anchor the parterre beds. Gravel pathways add the sense of sound to the garden as you walk through. It is important to invite and engage all the senses into the garden.

Feast among the Foxgloves

Feast among the Foxgloves

The lessons gardeners learn from their gardens are wonderful guiding principles for life. In an ever faster paced world, the tempo of nature is reassuring. Falling back into the natural order and rhythms of a garden and its subsequent timeline is in the very pulse of a gardener. Life presents marvelous moments to cherish and celebrate. The blooming of a flower, the birth of a child, the height of a season or the simplicity of a fine day all may inspire us to celebrate. It is the garden and its offerings that continually encourage me.

PRECEDING OVERLEAF LEFT: The parterre walls and pigeonniers are painted a soft, warm white, echoing the painted brick on Farmdale. The center bed is constructed of the same brick as the foundation of the home and the pathways. This is landscape architecture 101: bringing the architecture into the landscape, creating continuity and rhythm.

PRECEDING OVERLEAF RIGHT, CLOCKWISE FROM TOP LEFT: The morning sun making the foxgloves glow. Peach outdoor fabric on the McKinnon and Harris chairs mimics the peach and green color scheme of the garden. That vignette is my favorite place for morning coffee or afternoon tea. The garden gate beckons you into the garden and down the path.

ABOVE: In the steeple bed, white foxgloves bolt from a collar of chartreuse euphorbia, sage-hued sedum and silvery-toned lamb's ear. Pops of coral beckon beyond in the form of bright, salmon geraniums.

OPPOSITE: A specimen or two of "Best in Show" in clay pots can be moved as accents around the garden.

Feast among the Foxgloves

Feast among the Foxgloves

PRECEDING OVERLEAF LEFT: I love to set up a bar or buffet with one of the pigeonniers as the backdrop. They serve as great "bar backs" for extra supplies, and the complement of architecture and tablescape is visually pleasing.

PRECEDING OVERLEAF RIGHT: A simple cheese board and champagne is a go-to in my entertaining repertoire—it simply does the work for you! The season's first garden roses from my dear friend Mary Royal echo the peachy shades of the foxgloves.

ABOVE: Apricot, peach, salmon and coral all boast their floral splendor in the springtime garden at Farmdale.

OPPOSITE: A simple buffet of wine, cheese, champagne and fruit is a delightful springtime menu. My potted foxgloves make for perfect centerpieces on the buffet.

Feast among the Foxgloves

OPPOSITE: My grandmother's punch bowl is so multipurpose! I use punch bowls for centerpieces, for icing down wine or, well, for serving punch! It's the repurposing of heirlooms that gives them value today; they don't need to be used just for their original, intended function. I enjoy working with complementary textures like silver and glass, wicker and wood, potted specimens and cut flowers.

ABOVE: A twist on a traditional tiramisu, my Strawberry Tiramisu uses fresh strawberry jam between the layers of ladyfingers and whipped mascarpone. Just substitute strawberry jam for the espresso in your favorite tiramisu recipe.

OVERLEAF: It's the unexpected pop of a color or simply amazing flavor of a dish that makes a buffet or event truly memorable—whether it's salt on a chocolate chip cookie, creamy vanilla ice cream with warm cobbler, or a colorful bouquet in shades a touch brighter of the theme at hand. These yellow roses with melon, chartreuse and soft apricot undertones were the perfect complement to the buffet.

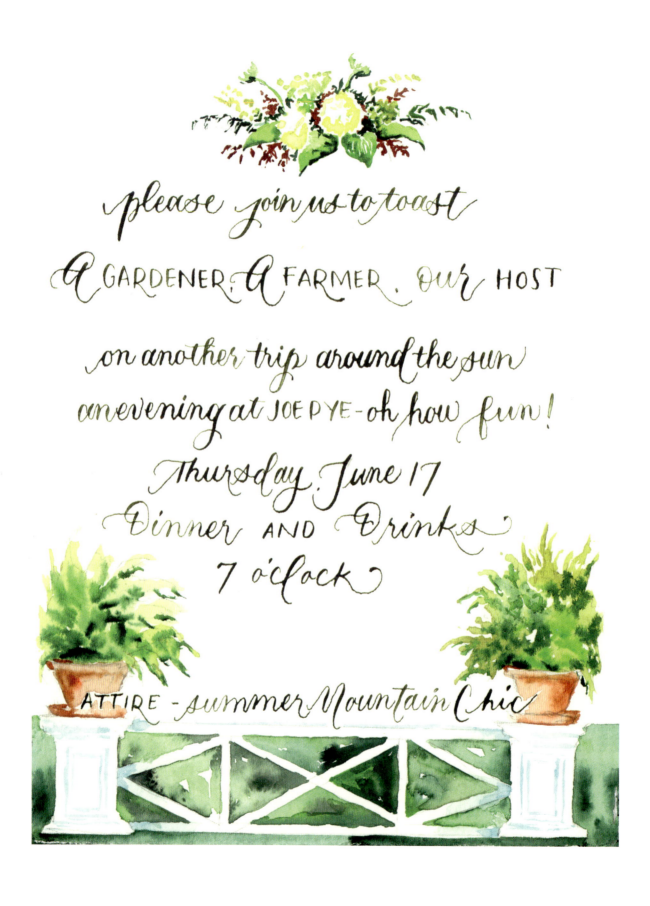

Birthday Dinner in Cashiers

Birthday Dinner in Cashiers

A true gift for me is to entertain at home—even for my birthday party! Setting the table, cutting flowers from the garden, cooking some best-loved dishes, and being able to work the angles of creativity therein is a favored occasion. My birthday is at the onset of the summer, and the produce and flowers of the season are starting to fill the farmers markets and our gardens. Inspiration comes in the form of a flavor or flower, a texture or tone or even that threshold crossed when the anticipation for something becomes reality—such as a birthday or the changing of a season.

Spring at home in the Deep South is a riot of color. A celebratory far cry from the grayness of winter. As we Southerners begin our trek into Appalachia for the summer, we find another spring awaits us. I hold true the thought that altitude directly effects my attitude, and I can feel my blood pressure dropping with each measured rise in the altitude. This "other spring," as I call it, awaits me in the mountains of North Carolina in June. Summertime has commenced its cadence of heat and humidity, but in the mountains, June is still mild.

Warm days are bookended by cool mornings and evenings. Ferns and hostas have emerged from the underground and made the forests lush again with fronds and foliage of varying greens and variegation. The mountain laurel has faded from pink to white and the canopy of the trees now shades the architectural branches recently exposed by the fall and winter.

This ever-verdant summer landscape amid the "other spring" is refreshing and inspires my entertaining to mimic and bend toward it. I bring my geraniums up the mountain to "summer camp" so they may enjoy the warm days and cool nights—faring better than the long, hot days back home. Thus, my mountain garden becomes colorful with the corals and salmons of the geraniums and roses of spring, much like Farmdale a month or two earlier.

Bringing some of the summer's first zinnias and dahlias with me up the mountain, I give my summertime home a foretaste of the glorious summer to come. Arranged with hosta leaves, basil and Queen Anne's Lace pods, a trio of bouquets serves as the centerpieces of my table. I love to have bouquets "marching" down a table, interposed with votives and candles.

As the saying in the mountains goes, "You can plan a pretty picnic, but you can't predict the weather." I sometimes have to move my table from the deck to underneath the deep eaves of the porch, as a summer shower is often a sure bet. I love switching things up, moving furniture around and giving a twist to the traditions of dinners past. My porch has panels of a brown and white buffalo check that can be drawn if the

Birthday Dinner in Cashiers

rain begins to "fall sideways," as I used to say when I was younger, when the wind steers the rainfall. When the panels are drawn, the porch becomes a cozy cocoon, and when they are open, the night breezes off the mountain are a welcomed element to the party. Potted ferns, ficus and gardenia topiaries add ambiance and love their summertime perch for the season. Older tables serve as bars and buffets when entertaining on the porch, weathering with each season and adding memories to their patina.

The color palette of green and white is always right! That's my motto! It works for the garden landscape and the tablescape, too. I am always finding inspiration at my friend Sandy's shop, Fiddlehead Designs. This time it was a tablecloth that I knew fit my adage and would be a wonderful base for the dinner table.

The tablecloth, an inky fern frond motif with coordinating napkins, is draped across my "beer garden" tables. Dozens of shades of greens can be found in this cloth, and I love to use it all summer long. The two tables can be pulled together for one long table and they work well as individual tables or as a table and serving board, bar or buffet. I delight in having pieces and locales that can serve double duty—multipurposing is a wonderful quality for entertaining! A pair of vintage iron chairs serve as the host and hostess chairs, and their scrollwork reminds me of fern tendrils and fronds unfurling. The Schumacher Greek key motif on the seat bottoms is an outdoor fabric I use at Farmdale and Joe Pye, another double duty use of a décor that can work here, there and just about anywhere!

Bamboo flatware, gold etched votives with ferns and waxy stick candles add an earthiness to the tabletop. Green and blue basketweave plates by Provvista Designs are juxtaposed with a mixture of glassware from crystal to celadon-hued to blown. Leafy greens, sage, chartreuse, and olive are set off by the white zinnias and dahlias—I rely on chartreuse to always come through and be the element in this color scheme to make things pop!

My longtime friend and fellow gardener, Drew English, is also one of the best cooks I know. He grows the most gorgeous dahlias, and any chance I am invited to dine at his table is a treat. Since it was my party, after all, I recruited Drew to handle the buffet. We schemed over some of our favorite Southern classics for summertime soirées and gave them a twirl on their tradition. From the charred lemon that gives panzanella pizazz, to peaches layered in a traditional Caprese salad, to roasted radishes accompanying a pork roast, I relished the chance to carry on a tradition yet add my own take . . . well, Drew's take, more so!

PRECEDING OVERLEAF: One thing to count on in Cashiers is an impromptu rain shower. The surrounding national forest, altitude and geography make the weather as unpredictable as can be. To be safe, my birthday dinner was under the porch. And, in fact, it did rain! But the sound was a perfect serenade for the meal.

OPPOSITE: I like to set up a buffet and let my friends fix their plates. My dear friend Drew English prepared a feast! It was my birthday, after all, so I wasn't the chef that day.

Birthday Dinner in Cashiers

OPPOSITE: Green and white is always right! Any season or setting, I love this classic combo. Here, shades of chartreuse mingle with verdant foliage. Zinnias, hosta leaves, bolted basil and Queen Anne's lace pods bloom out of trumpet vases. Touches of gold, warm bamboo, crystal glasses and white linens carry on the summery palette.

ABOVE LEFT: Cecilia's Cake Shop in Athens, Georgia, is a longstanding source for Georgians' celebratory cakes. My favorite, the Spanish Lemon cake, is perfect anytime of the year. Thankfully, Athens is the halfway point between Farmdale and Joe Pye Cottage, so why not make a pit stop?

ABOVE RIGHT: Homemade vanilla ice cream with a gardenia garnish. The essence of the scent flavors the ice cream. Cold silver punch cups add to the sensational dessert.

Birthday Dinner in Cashiers

OPPOSITE: Looking down the table toward the garden, where pops of white mountain laurel dot the understory of the forest canopy late into June. The green and white tablescape was truly inspired by the forest in early summer. The first of the summer dahlias dot the bouquets arrayed the length of the table, while the scrollwork of the end chairs remind me of fiddleheads.

ABOVE: My Aunt "Bee" has the most beautiful dinnerware (Provvista Designs) in varying shades of white, green and blue. Bamboo flatware pairs perfectly with the woven majolica basketweave of the dishes. The Italian linens were found at a favorite shop in Cashiers, Fiddlehead Designs. Fern fronds on the linens and votives echo the fern gullies just beyond the porch.

Birthday Dinner in Cashiers

One of the best gifts one can bestow on oneself is to delegate when entertaining. Don't become stressed or overwork yourself before a dinner party—have a bakery make your favorite cake! For me, the Spanish lemon cake by Cecelia's Cake Shop in Athens, Georgia, is an ultimate splurge. Though I would not typically put lemon desserts at the top of my list, this cake is truly divine—lemon done right with the perfect icing and layers of cake too! The lemon curd between the delicious layers is topped with a fluffy meringue icing—sweet and tart and textured beautifully. Gardenia-scented ice cream accompanied the cake, giving that heavenly Southern scent to creamy scoops of vanilla.

And, rather than playing bartender at my own party, I made a Peach Paloma base, to which my guests could add more or less of their preference—some with more fizz, others less, etc. Before-dinner drinks were taken into the garden, while the finishing touches were prepared on the meal. My preferred evening of this sort is to have a cocktail hour and dinner served buffet style with second helpings encouraged, and a dessert keeping the feast going well after the meal is finished. Wine at the table paired with the dinner relinquished one less decision, too. I think I inherited this from my mother, but that lingering moment after the dinner and dessert, when there is talking and laughing as the candles burn down, is probably my favorite moment at a dinner party.

In a time when so many things are hurried and rushed, the luxury of lingering is a treasure for sure. The gift of time, to yourself and to your friends and family is a precious gift. It's a gift not given lightly, but a trove to be cherished and stored deep within our hearts and minds. I am immeasurably blessed by these dinners of these good and perfect gifts.

OPPOSITE: The view of the table toward the buffet. Mixing faintly tinted, seeded lowball glasses with stemmed crystal wine glasses is part of the wonderful juxtaposition that gives the tablescape some je ne sais quoi. Mixing high and low is a design principle I follow for tables, homes and gardens.

Birthday Dinner in Cashiers

Birthday Dinner in Cashiers

PRECEDING OVERLEAF: The buffet is a feast of Southern summertime bounty. In the South, dinner is a celebratory meal, such as a Sunday midday meal, Christmas dinner, holiday or birthday proper. A supper is an evening meal. For a High Hampton birthday dinner, Drew cooked a spread of some favorites—Georgia Caprese Salad and Georgia Panzanella (peaches included with the tomatoes), fresh corn, wedges of watermelon and a pork roast.

OPPOSITE: The colors of summer in tomatoes and peaches and watermelon. Simply prepared and dressed food is my favorite kind! My dear friend Marianne Mebane keeps me stocked with a balsamic vinegar from her favorite Italian grocery store in New York, and that dressing is all the Georgia Caprese Salad needs.

I had never roasted radishes before I had them for dinner at Drew and Philip's house one night. A late-spring crop coming into the mountains, radishes are found at our local farmers market and stands. Roasting them caramelizes their sugars, creating a sweet and savory flavor that pairs perfectly with roasted pork.

ABOVE: One of my absolute favorite dishes is a Georgia Panzanella. Drew used cornbread croutons to soak up the vinegary dressing, and the peaches add a brightness along with the season's first 'maters. Grilled lemon is a tangy accompaniment along with the basil. This is a dish I can eat as a meal in and of itself. Sometimes I serve it with grilled chicken or a filet of salmon for a summertime supper.

Birthday Dinner in Cashiers

PRECEDING OVERLEAF LEFT: Before the dinner was set, my buffet on the porch doubled as a bar. Tea and water and a good white wine were perfect for this event. I love a late afternoon meal that carries into the evening but doesn't run too late. Then I'm still in bed early!

PRECEDING OVERLEAF RIGHT: My dear friend Margaret made a seasonal splash for us to sip on while the showers stopped and we could view the garden. Peach juice with a fresh twist of lime is a lovely, refreshing drink completed with gin and St. Germain. We called it a "Georgia Gimlet."

OPPOSITE: A view into the garden down the stepping stone path. The laurel wood arbor hosts a climbing hydrangea. Ajuga, a favored ground cover between step stones, is right at home at Joe Pye and Farmdale. This variety is called 'Chocolate Chip'.

ABOVE LEFT: My salmon geraniums from Farmdale take a trek northward to "summer camp" at Joe Pye. The longevity of the Middle Georgia heat wears on them, and they bloom all summer long in Cashiers, loving the cooler evenings. In fact, who doesn't love cool, mountain summertime evenings?

The anchor of the garden is a faux bois bench found at a local antique store. Standards of deep pink roses flank the bench and bloom all summer long.

ABOVE RIGHT: Another standard—a tree-form plant—is a variegated willow. The green-and-white leaves tipped with soft pink add variegation, too. Potted geraniums encircle the willow standard. Faux bois mushrooms "sprout" from the planter. These are some of my favorite doses of whimsy, found at the Gardener's Cottage, Asheville.

PLEASE JOIN ME FOR

Cocktails & Caladiums

SATURDAY, JULY 31

6 O'CLOCK

DINNER TO FOLLOW

~ ATTIRE ~

The garden is Dressed in her Summer Best

Follow her Lead... Green and White is Always Right

Summer Caladium Garden

Summer Caladium Garden

There is something solidly summer about July and August for us in the Deep South. These two months are not shared, split or spliced with spring as June can be, or flirted with by fall as September can be. These two months are summertime pure and simple. Hot, humid and lush!

Springtime brings peaches and pinks with foxgloves and geraniums, which are then repeated in the fall with sassanquas and mums in similar shades. For summertime, however, I keep a color palette of green and white in the garden, as it is not only visually bracing but refreshing amid the near tropical temps of my hometown in summer. Foliage and ferns are accented with begonias, hydrangeas, crepe myrtles and the stars of the summer garden, caladiums. Even if it's just a psychological trick, green and white is cooling to the eye if not the body.

A major gardening lesson I learned as a child was about bulbs and the magical mystery of them! I planted bulbs on our farm—onions, daffodils, caladiums and gladiolus—and was amazed that these papery-husked tubers, knobby and knotted looking, would produce not only sustenance but also flowers galore, and my favorite summer leaves—caladiums! As a young boy, my grand bazaar was the Ace Hardware in town (and it still is) for anything and everything I could ever hope for, need or want. Caladium bulbs in red, white, pink and mixed grab bags rested in bins of wood shavings, awaiting planting and my horticultural experimentation.

Plant the bulbs when the ground is still cool, and they just sit there! Let the soil warm (for us, Mother's Day or mid-May is ideal) and they pop up in June and last until October. I love the greens and whites of the speckled, dappled leaves, the strappy foliage, the broad elephant ear on display and the lime greens with dots of coral, or "carl" as Mama used to say, in the 'Miss Muffet' variety. Over the years, the solidly green and white varieties still make the chicest show in my garden.

As with the foxgloves, a dinner simply to observe the height of a season is reason enough to celebrate. A long table, candlelight, a setting sun, and the bounty of the garden as the centerpiece and backdrop is truly delightful and romantic. That combo of delight and romance is needed to break the daily routine that bustles around us at a frenetic pace. Just as a green and white color palette can be refreshing to the eye, so can a change of pace—or place—for a dinner party.

A chilled cantaloupe and mint gazpacho, hearty bread with butter blended with peach jam, crisp wine and lemonade are lighter fare for this seasonal supper and reminiscent of the garden's bounty. Drinks by the pool start and end the supper and somehow are connected to a late-night swim party too!

Summer Caladium Garden

My summer garden is a boyhood dream come true in adulthood. Those caladium bulbs planted under trees and in clay pots back then are still there for the choosing today. Farmdale's material selection and paint colors are mimicked in the garden structures and landscape architecture with the pigeonnier's palette, my outdoor furniture and the peachy hues of the brick and gravel. This accent of repetition—slightly varying from surface and plane, garden and home—is a design trick that creates a rhythm in our minds and for our eyes. Just as notes are assembled and played, colors also become a harmony. Green and white caladiums amid the verdant garden foliage create a restorative sensation. The open gate leads us into the garden proper, and each sense is invited to the season.

Creating a table in a setting like the garden is a favorite pastime. I relish the chance to show off the caladiums' hard work—after all, they're the ones in the heat all day—and effortlessly create an elegant tableau. I joke that I am a "lazy gardener, but a smart Farmer." I plant the plants that do the work for me—that thrive in my zone and garden—and, in turn, I applaud their accomplishments. An easy fait accompli for each season and a dinner party or two in the garden is reward aplenty.

PRECEDING OVERLEAF: Summer is in high swing. A long table set on the back lawn amidst the nodding caladiums is the setting for a garden dinner party. The verdant foliage, grass and lushness of the garden set off the crisp white linens and dinnerware for this event.

OPPOSITE: Gathered bunches of hydrangeas, hosta leaves, Liriope spikes and bolted basil adorn the table as a cadre of bouquets. For summertime, not only are green and white always right, but also blue and white. Anything to keep the effect cool. One of my all-time favorite color combos is peach and brown. Here, tortoiseshell goblets and flatware complement peachy-hued linens and the fruit.

Summer Caladium Garden

OPPOSITE: Large glass hurricanes cast a romantic glow as only candlelight can. Peaches scattered down the table reinforce the season. The hydrangeas are at their "antique" stage, probably my favorite look. The colors have become more jewel toned and saturated. The rich, lavender-blue color of these mopheads is a direct reflection of the soil pH where they are grown in my yard.

ABOVE: A chilled cantaloupe soup (befitting the color scheme) is the starter course for this alfresco summertime supper. Served with prosciutto, a hearty loaf of bread and mozzarella, it's practically a meal. The classic pairing of prosciutto and melon is lovely during this season.

OVERLEAF: The entrance to the garden. The cinnamon bark of the crepe myrtle is echoed in the tones of the cedar shake roofs, earthen-hued brickwork and gravel. A Chippendale bench in light blue keeps the cooler palette and is visually delightful. 'Miss Muffet' caladiums nod and bow in the slightest breeze or simply when walked past, which makes them perfect greeters for garden visitors in the summer. I love their chartreuse foliage and hot pink "freckles."

PRECEDING OVERLEAF: The steeple bed in all its summer grandeur. The juicy sedum has sprouted and the flowers are a deeper, rusty pink—a sign of the next season to come. Pots of white geraniums and scaevola dot the corners and edges of the parterre walls. The garden receives full sun from late morning into mid-afternoon, but the shade of the loquats creates the perfect spot for caladiums. This variety is 'Grey Ghost' and grows up to three feet tall, spilling over the hedges by summer's end.

ABOVE: Some plants, like the caladiums, simply do the work for you as long as you plant them where they won't "complain." Sedums and succulents are also such plants, simply thriving in the heat. Ajuga, too, loves the sun and heat, and this variety, 'Burgundy Glow', picks up on the soft lavenders in the succulents.

OPPOSITE: The morning light from the east starts to make the caladiums glow. Dew droplets dance on the leaves and puddle in their centers. Caladiums were one of the first plants I ever planted and learned about. Their metamorphosis from bulb to plant is quite stunning and fascinating to me still! The awe I felt as a child learning about plants is still a part of me today.

Summer Caladium Garden

Summer Caladium Garden

PRECEDING OVERLEAF: The green and white of the painted brick, shutters and doors is echoed in the planting scheme. Here, the four parterres are brimming with caladiums in their summertime splendor. The parterre garden is in the shape of a "Celtic Cross" with the crossbars punctuated with a circle. Geometry reinforced with landscape architecture is always a visual delight.

LEFT: A diagonal view across the parterres reveals the wall fountain and one of the pigeonniers through the loquat limbs. My garden is truly an extension of my home. I entertain here. My sister was married in this garden. Celebrations grand and small have been hosted amidst these hedges and plantings. From my morning coffee in the garden to a nightcap while watching fireflies, my garden is one of my favorite rooms of my home. In summer, the whiz of hummingbirds, buzz of bees and chatter from dozens of birds serenade me. Burbling water in a fountain adds to the symphony.

OVERLEAF: The front façade of Farmdale is flanked by two standard crepe myrtles, which bloom simultaneously with the caladiums at their summer peak in the back garden. Pots of 'Miss Muffet' caladiums are placed around the syrup kettle fountain, all bubbling out of a bed of chartreuse creeping Jenny. A herringbone brick walkabout borders the front lawn and guides my guests to the front door. Robert Norris, of the firm Spitzmiller and Norris, designed my home.

September Charm

September Charm

A recipe and ratio of the best—three parts summer, one part fall. You can give or take either ingredient to your liking depending on your locale.

September is a collision of so many wonderful things in the mountains. Summer and fall jostle each other and so does their produce. Peaches and pumpkins, apples and tomatoes, summer squashes and their autumnal cousins—it's a spectacular time of year! Officially, summer ends and fall begins this month, and it's simply unapologetic about this seasonal slam.

For me, one of the best aspects of this month is the weather. Warm days, cool nights—and a flirtation of fall while summer is still handing out flowers, fruit and full foliage. Hikes and pickleball are perfect during the day and a fire and a good dinner in the evening augments the day superbly.

Two stars from the flower garden are the sunflowers and hydrangeas. The paniculata species have turned from white to shades of pink, crimson, chartreuse, coral, rusty reds and every shade in between. Plus, now is the perfect time to dry them, too. Just clip them once they've changed from their summer whites into chartreuse and pinky shades of autumn and arrange in place—easy breezy!

Sunflowers reinforce their name with their sunny disposition and terrific, jaunty color. Yellow is fabulous this month and sets off the hydrangeas and foliage starting to turn. I love to grow sunflowers in the garden, too. Repeat blooming ones take the place of typical mums; perennial "swamp" sunflowers are garden show-offs this season as well.

In September, a second round of sunflowers starts coming into the farmers markets and floral shops. These stems are full of character and pizazz! Arranged in honey-hued pottery, bouquets saunter down my table on the deck, interposed with wicker and etched glass hurricanes. The sunlight this time of year is repeated in the sunflowers, and then mimicked in the dinnerware and threads of the napkins. Punctuation of contrasts—like glass and wicker, rattan and linen, and further taken to the menu—adds to delight of any occasion.

Fried chicken dinners are a Southern Sunday tradition, and I like to entertain on Sunday afternoons and evenings, starting with drinks in the garden followed by supper on the deck. And why not? The weather is absolutely perfect for these alfresco celebrations!

Something I've learned through my entertaining adventures is that folks like what they like—especially when it comes to the bar. If she likes wine, she's going to drink wine! If he prefers a G&T, that's what he'll have! A stocked bar gives your guests that autonomy to make their drink of choice, but another adage I live

September Charm

PRECEDING OVERLEAF: September in the mountains is a season within a season, a recipe of the best ratios from summer and fall. One of my absolute favorite things about this month is when the hydrangeas turn pink. Pots of 'SunBelievable' sunflowers take me from late summer into fall. I think the color combo of yellow and pink is just perfect in this month.

OPPOSITE: Mixed varieties of sunflowers and some hydrangeas make a showstopper centerpiece for the bar set in the garden. Their "vase" is a vintage brass bamboo cache pot. As my friend Margaret says, "If it can hold ice, it can be a wine cooler." Hence the use of white wicker-pattern ceramic planters. A colorful tablecloth mimics the turning of leaves that is just around the corner.

ABOVE LEFT: A pair of terra-cotta razorbacks serve as sentries in the garden; I delight in a touch of whimsy or something unexpected. The hydrangeas start to turn pink and nearly red, while ferns are still lush and verdant.

ABOVE RIGHT: From geraniums in the summer to sunflowers in the fall, I love watching the seasons change—and what better place than the North Carolina mountains, where one can almost have all four seasons in a day!

September Charm

by is to have one signature drink to get the party started and for those who feel adventuresome or who are simply undecided. I always have a tray of the signature drink awaiting my guests upon arrival. This time of year, as the peaches are on their way out, my drink creation salutes their glorious season one last time!

Like any good Southern boy worth his grits, I've sliced and "put up" peaches, but freezing them is perfect for this drink. Blend frozen peaches with a bit of simple syrup, flavor it with mint or basil, add a pour of a favorite liquor and you have a cocktail! Refreshing and delicious, this drink can be mixed further with tea, served with cheese straws and even made ahead for easy prep. The color is gorgeous, fitting with the sunflowers and linens, and truly does the work for you!

Entertaining and hosting is a selfish endeavor for me. I enjoy it! This is an opportunity to take inventory of my china and serving pieces, add and subtract what I do and don't need, collect and create, gather with friends and celebrate the essence of each season. I enjoy cooking and feeding folks at my table, and other times, I enjoy having it catered. The joy in entertaining is its own reward. Since I can set a table, arrange flowers and combine flavors in much shorter time than it takes to design a house, my creative itch is scratched and nearly instant gratification is granted for all the things I love.

When designing a client's home, I often use the expression "salt on a chocolate chip cookie." It's the contrast of flavors that accentuates the stronger flavor—the salt making the chocolate's profile brighter and richer but giving our palates the diverse flavors of a sweet and salty meeting. That's what this particular season is about to me. The best of seasons kiss in September and it's worthy of celebration!

OPPOSITE: Woven and wicker, rattan and bamboo—wonderful textures for entertaining pieces. The color combo of yellow, salmon and raffia is perfect for this season. Vicki Miller pottery, from Vivian Metzger antiques in Cashiers, is the loveliest shade of Dijon and boasts the jauntiness that sunflowers portray.

OVERLEAF: Woven wicker flatware and glassware, echoed in the hurricanes and coasters, is a classic theme for late summer and fall. The texture and sentimentality of woven elements and baskets is quintessential to the mountain style. From picnics to fly-fishing to gathering apples, I appreciate the earthiness of woven baskets and similar pieces. Some of the season's first apples dot the table along with a few leaves of mountain laurel and rhododendron. Initial Reaction in Perry found the perfect marigold thread for these stitched napkins.

September Charm

RIGHT: A view from the porch to the deck shows the table basking in the September sun. I keep a table and chairs on this end of the deck at Joe Pye for easy access to the grill and porch. I can serve from a buffet under the porch or on the deck. Painted wooden barrels are bursting with Kimberly Queen ferns and 'Diamond Frost' euphorbia. I plant them in May and they last until Thanksgiving. An old grape-harvesting metal bucket is now a planter for a Japanese maple. I relish when this maple turns golden yellow and fades to an orange through the fall.

OVERLEAF: A play on a Sunday dinner, a menu of chicken and biscuits, a green salad and roasted tomatoes makes for a delicious meal. A honey bourbon fig cake is dessert. When entertaining, I enjoy preparing the simpler sides myself but rely on a local secret for the main course: a local gas station serves up the best chicken tenders, and grocery store bakery biscuits are just fine! Dressed with hot honey or peach jam, these biscuits are a winner winner chicken dinner any season!

Little things can elevate the everyday, such as the jam or honey, or even a homemade mayo for the tomatoes—and take the celebration up a notch. If you're going to the trouble of making homemade mayonnaise, then gas station chicken tenders are totally acceptable!

September Charm

ABOVE: The juxtaposition of the horizontal lines of the tablecloth and the lines of the chairs and railings makes for fun geometry. I enjoy entertaining from this perch on my deck. Whether it's a formal affair or grilled burgers, the backdrop within the canopy of the trees and the mountain air make the memories truly wonderful.

OPPOSITE: Local beekeeper Rose Mary Achy makes the most fabulous cake from her bees' honey. I don't know what the bees are eating at Calm Creek, her farm outside Cashiers, but this is truly some of the best honey I've ever had. Rose Mary's Honey Bourbon Cake is nothing short of divine. Fresh figs from the Cashiers Farmers Market add a late summer element to the cake. I use Calm Creek Honey in my tea, for cooking and any chance I can.

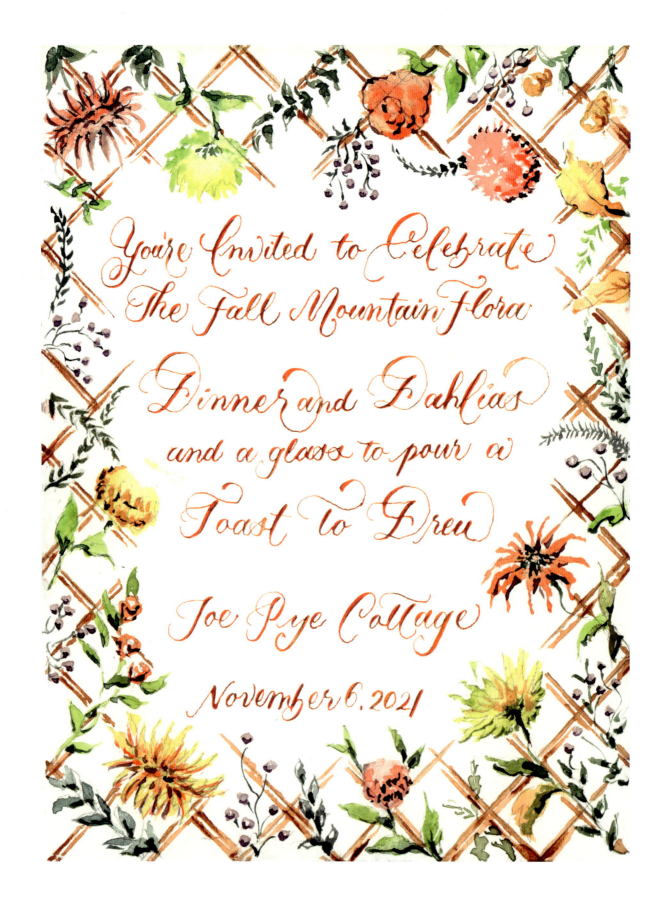

Dahlia Dinner

Dahlia Dinner

A few things I have learned as a gardener and host are to cater what you cannot cook and glean what you cannot grow! I refer to myself as a lazy gardener, as I grow a few things that love their growing conditions in my gardens, and I grow many of those particular things. If one caladium works, a hundred work even better! I take the same approach with foxgloves and zinnias too.

I absolutely adore dahlias. Every shape and color, texture and petal formation, size and silly name is a wonder to me. But I cannot grow them. I have tried. And I have retried. Once you see the dahlias grown by my friends Mary Royal in Perry and Drew English in Cashiers, you too will resign your efforts and patronize their handiwork. I'll gladly set the table, arrange the flowers and host a dahlia dinner—just don't expect me to grow them!

For generations, dahlia dinners in and around Cashiers have been the culmination of the summer season and a toast to the coming fall. Held in late September or early October, before the frost takes the dahlias down and out, these dinners are celebrations of the season to come but really are a commemoration of the passing summer—a time when friends and family reunite in the cool mountain climate and reminisce on the joy of summertime in the mountains. Toasts are made in memory, honor and anticipation.

Setting up the table on the deck, the background is a scenic, autumn wonderland. Rusts and coppery leaves glow above the darker greens of the rhododendron and mountain laurel. Highlights of amber and scarlet leaves are offset by the seemingly honey-infused light. A favorite tablecloth of gourds, pumpkins, figs and fall foliage sets the stage for the tablescape. Red- and mustard-glazed pottery by Vicky Miller brims with dahlias, the showstopping raison d'etre for this festive time. Nandina berries, persimmons and orange roses fill the pottery too—complete with accents of fall leaves. This series of bouquets creates a hedge of gorgeous flowers parading down the entire table.

A painted series of game fauna and fowl serves as the dinnerware, while ruby red seeded glass goblets mix with vintage game bird lowball glassware. A caramel-check napkin and natural-toned bamboo flatware add an earthen element and color to the tableau. Amber and gold etched-glass votives reflect and refract their firelight and mimic the autumnal setting sun through the foliage.

I use my porch and deck together when entertaining outside in the mountains. The drier fall air allows this setup to be more practical for dining than during the summertime with its pop-up showers. I like to use the porch as the beginning, middle and end—setting up the bar, buffet and dessert—and giving my guests a bit of a progressive dinner between the garden and the house. Starters

Dahlia Dinner

such as my favorite seasoned crackers and a festive cocktail allow us to gather on the porch and begin the evening. Setting up the buffet on the porch is convenient, as we pass through on the way to the dinner table. Afterward, dessert can be served on the porch or back at the table—whatever encourages my guests to enjoy and linger longer into the evening.

I love my porch throughout the seasons, but fall is exceptionally nice. The potted ferns are full and flowing to the ground from their perches. Potted begonias with resplendent amethyst leaves truly set off the other colors. I am mesmerized by purples, lavenders and plum tones in the fall. The bar arrangement is a cornucopia of fall flowers and foliage—oak, maple and magnolia; limelight hydrangeas boasting their tinges of pink and red; and branches of castor bean showing off their brilliant ruby seed pods—and anchors one end of the porch.

Often, I like to serve two desserts—a chocolate one of course, and a seasonally inspired sweet treat. For this dahlia dinner, I relied on the fabulous culinary skills of my dear friend and neighbor Karen Hirons.

Toasting to the dahlias and the season they represent is a wonderful tradition I am honored to uphold.

PRECEDING OVERLEAF: As with the garden, the porch is another room for my home. Outdoor fabrics are used for the upholstery and working panels between the posts. In case of wind or rain, the panels can be pulled and the porch becomes a wondrously cozy perch. The table in front of the panel wall is my buffet and bar. I like to create large, seasonal arrangements against the backdrop and underneath the vintage sign.

The exaggerated buffalo check is by Stroheim and the "Elsie" fern motif by Scalamandré, seen on lumbar pillows and lampshades. My late dog, Sampson, loved the porch at Joe Pye Cottage.

OPPOSITE: Red seeded-glass goblets, vintage lowball tumblers and a mix of pottery add festive flair to the Dahlia Dinner tablescape. Roses, nandina berries, persimmons and, of course, dahlias are all arranged in pottery vases by Vicki Miller.

OVERLEAF: Painted hunting scenes on the Provvista Designs dinnerware is a favorite choice for place settings. Bamboo flatware is light and fun. The tablecloth, a find from Fiddlehead Designs in town, depicts heirloom pumpkins and fall foliage set in a tendril trellis. Caramel-check napkins are stitched in black, and Initial Reaction monogrammed my initials in a fishtail style using the same thread. A collection of pottery vases creates a "hedge" down the table for the dahlias interposed with season foliage and other flowers. My friend Eliza Price painted the place cards.

PRECEDING OVERLEAF, LEFT AND RIGHT: Drew English grows the most exquisite dahlias for High Hampton. The culmination of his hard work is the Dahlia Dinner hosted at the end of the growing season amidst the dahlias—a High Hampton tradition. It's quite the spectacular event! This dinner inspired my Dahlia Dinner at Joe Pye later in the season for our group of pals in the mountains, including Drew. My favorite, Dahlia 'Henriette', is seen (right) in perfect splendor!

OPPOSITE: The two hosts. I loved entertaining in the mountains with Sampson by my side; he enjoyed a party. From the porch to the deck to the garden, any reason is reason enough to celebrate. The view from my porch to the deck and garden below is a favorite observation point, taking in the foliage beyond.

ABOVE: A vintage, rusty wire planter is one my favorite finds. I fill it with nods to the season. Here, old-fashioned chrysanthemums in the most glorious turmeric hue are complemented by variegated ivy. I have a fondness for baskets, plant stands and the like as welcoming gestures on the porch, deck or in the garden.

Dahlia Dinner

ABOVE: A feast for the eyes; after all, as Mimi said, "We eat with our eyes first!" My sweet friend Libby Endry, who also has a home nearby in Cashiers, created this whimsical arrangement from produce and foliage. The faux bois log planter is from her shop, Gardener's Cottage, where she also sells the seasoned crackers; I always have a bag on hand to serve with drinks on the porch.

OPPOSITE: The buffalo-check panels on the porch frame the dinner table on the deck. Another table serves as a secondary bar or dessert spot. I like displaying seasonal stems and limbs. Here, plumes of ornamental grasses mix with persimmons still on the stem. I like to have what I call "pull up" pieces for extra seating; an ottoman tucked under the table provides an extra perch when the porch is full.

OPPOSITE: I love to serve a "dessert heavy" meal in the fall. There are so many flavors and recipes, it's hard to pick just one! My neighbor and dear friend Karen Hirons brought her absolutely delicious Apple and Pear Galette, which she serves with crème fraîche. It's perfect served with coffee.

ABOVE: The bar is set with a large arrangement of seasonal branches. The bar at my favorite hotel in New York, the Lowell, always has the most fabulous stems and branches arranged. Imitation is flattery, the saying goes!

Dahlia Dinner

ABOVE: If you can turn on the oven, you can make bruschetta. Trust me! Here, slow-roasted tomatoes—still rolling in until the frost kills them—and garlic are spread like butter atop goat cheese on toast. Sometimes I make a meal out of this, adding a fried egg. The best and simplest note to this dish is to use coarse, flaky sea salt. It will change the way you eat toast and cheese—or anything!

OPPOSITE: A go-to starter is capered shrimp—simply boil the shrimp and dress in champagne vinegar, capers and some of their brine, and a hearty chopping of fresh dill. There's just something about gathering on the porch and having starters and good drinks in the mountain air that's my kind of party.

Dahlia Dinner

ABOVE: This salad is a wonderful fall dish that doesn't require any cooking. Sliced pears, crumbly, creamy blue cheese, candied walnuts and prosciutto are dressed with the slightest drizzle of olive oil. I pick up all the ingredients at the Farmers Market and assemble on a platter. After it has sat for a bit, the flavors meld together. A sprinkling of thyme leaves makes the dish truly fantastic. This salad was inspired by my friend Kristin Jorgensen, who teaches cooking classes at her barn out from town in Cashiers. I love her approach to seasonal dishes. Keep it fresh and simple, and the flavors work their magic!

OPPOSITE: My deck dining table and chairs are from an old biergarten in Germany. I found them at an antique shop in Asheville. I can fold and move them into the garden or under the porch easily. I have two tables end to end here, to seat more folks. I like to dress them so the corners hang down like pendants. The host and hostess chairs, which I painted a nearly perfect Kelly green to match the biergarten chairs, are old garden chairs I found at Turner's Antiques in Marshallville, Georgia, close to Perry.

OPPOSITE: My neighbor and friend Karen and I have both attended, and cannot wait to return to, Kristin Jorgensen's classes at The Barn. We learned this panna cotta recipe, which is an elegant yet simple dish that pairs perfectly with any seasonal fruit. Here, it is served with pears poached in a Sancerre wine. Candied lemon peel and mint make for the perfect garnishes.

ABOVE: A childhood friend and still best friend today, Jennifer aka "Red," has an allergy to gluten. She makes a flourless chocolate torte that is absolutely scrumptious! My neighbor Karen taught me the powdered sugar trick: set a leaf atop a dessert, dust with powdered sugar and voilà!

You're invited to enjoy

Wine in the Garden at Farmdale

NOVEMBER 21

FIVE IN THE AFTERNOON

FALL ALFRESCO CHIC ATTIRE

Alfresco Fall

Alfresco Fall

I repeat this every year, I have it printed on cocktail napkins and it has been quoted in books and magazines, "Fall is a Southerner's reward for surviving summer."

The autumnal season is truly glorious. October into November is gorgeous in the mountains, and then, the fabulousness of fall is extended well into November for the Deep South. Fall in the mountains is quintessentially the vision of the season. The leaves, the dahlias and mums, pumpkins and festivals and seemingly everything smells of cinnamon and warm spices. Fall has long been my favorite season, though I can make a case for praiseworthy highlights in every season. Within each season proper, there are moments that constitute the very best of that time of year, and the opportunity to celebrate is nothing short of magical.

There are "pocket seasons" in the South, as I refer to them, when you find a microseason set within the parameters of a season proper, where everything is just fantastical. It may be a day or two, a week, or a couple of weeks; it is short yet divinely appointed and worth commemorating. *Perfect*—a word not used lightly—describes these particularly polished moments that should be absorbed and cherished. We can hold dear the memories made within them to ponder in our hearts and minds when the seasons bring imperfect days.

This fall pocket season is somewhere from early to mid-November. The temperatures are finally constantly cool, while the days are still warm and enjoyable. A crispness has replaced the humidity; tea olives scent the air with their perfume; sassanquas begin to bloom and the light is ephemeral, fleeting but golden. The gardens are still verdant, but the Japanese maples have turned a mustardy gold, the dogwoods are a kaleidoscope of scarlet and ruby-hued tones, and the roses are finishing their season with what may be their best blossoms of the year. Nandina and holly berries are orange-to-red and every shade therein, and outdoor entertaining at this time is rivaled only by spring entertaining—but with the bonus of no pollen!

With the heaviness of the holidays and their menus approaching, I find myself wanting to mark this fall pocket with a menu extolling this ideal season within a season. Crisp dawns and cool dusks, with pleasantly warm days, call for cheese boards, pickle trays, perhaps a seasonal soup, and a crudités platters reflecting the color palette—each setting/laying a different course for the palate.

When I was in school, I remember a teacher giving us a history lesson on a "coup d'état." I raised my hand and told her that my Mimi could "fix" one! She "fixes them all the time!" Naturally, I was using the Southern lingo *fix*, which also means to prepare or cook, not just to repair. The teacher laughed and said that my grandmother was the reason for world peace! I still believe that to be true on some grounds . . . but I digress.

Alfresco Fall

Mimi often made crudités trays and platters to start a meal or as snacks for the family. Cheese and crackers with perhaps some pickles accompanied the crudités, and dips paired with these elements. I later learned that this snack or first course was an amazing ploy to get us to eat our veggies! Mimi's sauces of cream cheese and olives, or perhaps sour cream with dill—both simple and delicious—were the dips and spreads for carrots, celery, radishes, blanched green beans and sugar snap peas. As I grew up, I realized that a cheese board and a veggie tray can constitute a fabulous supper! A heady rosé to complement it, and a true celebration of the season is set, y'all!

Taking advantage of the golden hour's fleeting moments, I set a table in my garden by the fountain and another in the lawn as a buffet. The dining table is a riot of color and texture—a nod to the colorful autumnal foliage—that includes an homage to the last of the garden roses. Candlelight mimics the sunlight and carries the feast into the evening.

Glasses of wine and the first nibbles of the cheeses and vegetables begin the dinner, and my guests are encouraged to mill about the garden and soak up the setting sun through the trees. Following that, a soup and salad course rounds everything out. A creamy sweet potato bisque, garnished with crème fraîche and apples, keeps us toasty as the evening yields its warmth to the cooling night. Dessert of pumpkin poundcake and coffee is then served inside, keeping the evening's progression in play.

Simple, elegant meals such as this are applicable throughout all the seasons. But before the hectic schedules of the approaching holidays, a refreshing respite for a dinner party of friends to enjoy being together is reason enough to celebrate this enchanting pocket of time.

PRECEDING OVERLEAF: The setting sun sets the Japanese maples aglow with spectacular fall color. One of my favored meals is a symphony of salads and starters. The buffet is set in the garden against this lovely autumnal backdrop of sun and maples.

OPPOSITE: I keep a table and chairs by my wall fountain in the garden at Farmdale. It is my most often-used setting for alfresco suppers and dinners when not entertaining larger crowds. This table and chairs seat six perfectly, which is a good number to serve casually. My baby sister and her husband, as well as my aunt and uncle, live quite close; hence, the frequent off-the-cuff gatherings.

Alfresco Fall

PRECEDING OVERLEAF: Fall is unapologetic in its myriad tones, textures and tastes. Inspired by the colors in an Indian tablecloth, mixing vibrant jewel tones and fun patterns is reminiscent of the season's offerings. The last of the garden roses in deep shades of magenta, burgundy, ruby, garnet and goldenrod stand aside a large hurricane. My mother's stemware, in every jewel tone, mix with seeded lowball glasses. Brilliant emerald flatware atop the vibrant tablecloth and pumpkin-hued napkins are a charming play on a color scheme of which I am fond—peach and green.

RIGHT: The western path of the garden leads to the pool gate. The Japanese maples flank a faux bois bench. The light this time of year is nothing short of magical, so I try to entertain outside as much as I can.

OVERLEAF: Something for everyone: a fruit and cheese board, a trio of pickled items and a crudités platter. I'll serve a rosé or Sancerre with this spread. Two types of flora specimens serve as arrangements on the buffet: one a bouquet of garden roses arranged with nandina berries in shades of apricot, persimmon and terra-cotta; the other a rusty antique urn filled with angel vine and ajuga. I adore this duo, which grows wonderfully in the sun or shade, and often use it as accent pots around the garden. It serves double duty as a buffet arrangement with branches of arching Elaeagnus creating some height and drama.

Alfresco Fall

Alfresco Fall

Alfresco Fall

PRECEDING OVERLEAF LEFT: The fall foliage and setting sun make for a handsome, elegant backdrop to the pigeonniers and buffet.

PRECEDING OVERLEAF RIGHT: A seasonal soirée and very little cooking involved—blanching the asparagus if you wish! In this season of, as Mimi said, "heavy cooking" for the holidays, a platter of crudités is just the ticket to a simple yet elegant entertaining offering. The sour cream is mixed with salt and some fresh dill—it's the easiest dip and a perfect accompaniment to so much, from crudités to salmon!

LEFT: My friend Sara Jo McLean is a caterer extraordinaire. She says, "It's just in the way you slice it!" She makes the loveliest spreads for her family and guests. Whether it's star fruit, persimmons or wedges of oranges, she taught me to show off the fruit's best feature.

Another trick of the trade she shared with me is how to make a cheese log. Take goat cheese, dried cranberries and dried apricots, mix them together, and you have a spread worthy of toast, crackers, chicken breast or a salmon filet! Shape it into a log and voilà! Sara Jo's dates stuffed with cream cheese and a salted pecan are simply delicious too.

Friendsgiving in Cashiers

Friendsgiving in Cashiers

We have our friends and we have our family—and we have "framily," friends who are like family. Our holiday tables, proper, are often filled with our family members—immediate relations seated in the dining room and the kids relegated to card tables in the kitchen or picnic tables outside. A Friendsgiving dinner is the opportunity to entertain and celebrate our holidays with friends—in addition to, or in some cases, in place of, the tradition feast with family!

For a group of high school friends and mountain pals, I orchestrate a Friendsgiving in Cashiers in November. Once of my dearest friends, Lea, has a birthday in late October, and this is prime time to gather for a fall weekend with friends, have a birthday dinner and toast to many years of friendship.

A festive tablescape of fall flowers, foliage and colors is assembled with flairs of fun colors in glassware, pottery and dinnerware. Amethyst is such a glorious color for autumn. It sets off the saturated depths of rust, orange and scarlet while letting the brighter whites, creams and pastels have their moment, too. Wine goblets and ornamental cabbage dot the tablescape, creating rhythm with repetition, but giving the orange maple leaves, terracotta roses and rusty redwood some contrast and highlight.

Starting and ending the dinner in the living room with fireside cocktails, I set a bar on the table underneath my coral screen—the epicenter and inspiration for all colors at Joe Pye. I use silver julep cups through the year—the tangible, tactile feel of a cold drink in the summer or a warm one in the colder months is what the appeal of these cups is all about! Copper and pewter mules and mugs work great too!

After a glass of wine or preferred drink, we head into the dining room for the meal. Stick candles, with their waxy tendrils of bittersweet and bark relief, are lit—creating an ambiance that candlelight alone can create.

Around the living room at Joe Pye, I love to have small bouquets on the coffee table and large arrangements on the tables. A few branches of maple, pyracantha and nandina quickly set the seasonal flair and backdrop for the bar. A trick to the trade is drying hydrangeas on my mantel and other tables—clipping them in September when they have turned from white to soft pink and arranging them in place. A few magnolia branches and birch twigs liven up the mantel jars—giving a lovely, seasonal flair to the green glazed jugs. For the large pottery jug, made by my friend Charlie West, a simple array of cloudlike hydrangeas dries in place—set off simply by a bowl of bright, green apples fresh from the Cashiers Farmers Market.

Another trick of the trade when arranging flowers is to cluster small bouquets together. This collection creates a wonderful display! Use a brass or wooden tray to create a platform or corral for your bouquets and

Friendsgiving in Cashiers

Friendsgiving in Cashiers

Two seating areas encompass the living room at Joe Pye cottage. Between the two, against the large picture window, is a table that serves as the hyphen between the groupings. Charlie West, a Georgia potter, made the large vessel, which I fill with seasonal branches the moment I arrive in the mountains, truly bringing the outdoors inside! White ironstone tureens, something I collect, meld with the pottery and lamps, too, which Charlie originally made as vases.

The hydrangeas begin their transformation from white to lime green to russets and pinks in the fall and dry beautifully.

Friendsgiving in Cashiers

voilà! Their collective collaboration creates a wonderful centerpiece. I love how the dahlias, roses and bittersweet berries mimic the firelight. A silver dish of toasted nuts gives your guests something to munch while enjoying their fireside sips.

Pottery pumpkins and gourds by my friend Caroline Boykin are placed down the table. I love these gourds, as they are a perennial favorite to decorate with and work into a tablescape, mantel décor, as seasonal accents or anywhere they're placed. Their glaze and color works perfectly with the color scheme of my Friendsgiving tableau. I love the mix of high and low, old and new, found and forgotten—my dining room's color inspiration comes from a large Rose Medallion platter setting the tone.

Aquas and oranges, pink and pale greens, all take me through the seasons and inspire tablescapes throughout the year. The mix of handmade pottery with old porcelain is the collected feel that is a hallmark of Southern style. With generations of tableware and favorite finds, floral delights and seasonal nods, I love having my friends who are like my family at my table.

For a Friendsgiving meal, I usually stray away from the traditional Thanksgiving menu—serving a hearty soup and salad with artisanal bread. The real sustenance of these gatherings is the laughter and reunion of lifelong friends, the pleasure of making new acquaintances and the happy memories being created. I am so thankful for my friendships represented at my table, and always look forward to tasting and toasting with them each and every season.

OPPOSITE: A view into my dining room, set for a Friendsgiving feast! I love to use color in the mountains—persimmon, aqua, fern frond green—and bringing that kaleidoscope to the tabletop is reminiscent of the foliage and flowers of the season at hand.

OVERLEAF: The Estelle wine glasses in a scrumptious amethyst hue are a lovely complement to the fall tablescape. My sweet friend Caroline Boykin is a fabulous artist and potter who made the gourds seen nestled among the bouquets. Vintage brass bamboo flatware and hemstitched linens flank the place settings made by Tallahassee artist William Lamb depicting quail and hunting dogs.

OPPOSITE: Inspiration finds me in unexpected routes and places. I found the large rose medallion platter at an estate sale, and its colors—persimmon and jade and aqua—inspired the color scheme for my dining room. The Brunschwig and Fils plaid, mountain pottery, and a collection of tabletop items and serving pieces all have a hue, shade or tint found in the rose medallion platter. Branches of rhododendron add an element of the mountain landscape to the tableau.

ABOVE: Sometimes the best flowers aren't actually flowers at all! Ornamental cabbages are cut and arranged in vases along with roses and fall foliage. Amethyst, plum and deep purples are underrated, in my opinion, especially for the autumnal palette. They set off the brilliance of the other colors and add depth and richness. A collection of antique barley twist candle sticks from Vivianne Metzger Antiques hold Stick Candles, made locally in Highlands of 100 percent beeswax and poured into molds one at a time—fresh and fun! I think about the craftsmen who carved and turned the candlesticks over a century ago, and how their handiwork is celebrated and used today. Artists like Caroline Boykin continue to create and inspire; her gourds are seen here.

ABOVE: The warm patina of my buffet in the dining room is an agreeable contrast to the gilt mirror—both reflective of the Louis style. Majolica asparagus plates and colorful pottery lamps bring the room's palette to this vignette. All it takes is a stem, branch or blossom, and the season is celebrated. A couple of branches of amber-orange maple leaves are set off with bright green apples from the farmers market.

OPPOSITE: I adore a cross-section view of a table. Often, we are looking down and across; but just diagonally, the angle and view totally change. Looking toward the buffet, seeing the room reflected in the mirror, the vertical punctuation of the candles on the table is like a city skyline, the treeline of an approaching forest or mountain range in the distance. A fall tablescape is the perfect excuse to layer all the elements of the season and interpret autumn for your friends and family.

Friendsgiving in Cashiers

ABOVE: A trip to England reminded me so much of Cashiers. From the cottages and terrain to the foods and gardens, I felt right at home. Apple cider was in production when we were there and is the base for many a drink, cocktail and marinade too. Here, a spiked cider mixed with rosemary simple syrup and pear nectar is delicious served warm or cold. The cider at the Newt in Somerset inspired this concoction.

OPPOSITE: A drinks buffet, tucked underneath the stairs at Joe Pye, is home to "David," our resident bartender and vintage brass deer. We joke that David serves the spirits on the mountain. The carvings and hardware on this buffet are what drew me to it, but what I also love about antique pieces is how useful they are. The storage is ample, deep and at hand, as if this piece were designed and crafted for such a task! Using and thus celebrating antiques and heirlooms gives them renewal and repurposed vitality in our homes.

OVERLEAF: We love to play games after dinner next to the fire. Here, the deep pink hues of the season's dried hydrangeas mix with magnolia leaves and pods and birch twigs. The vintage ice buckets are from the old High Hampton Inn. Asheville artist Bee Sieberg painted the sheep. Having my friends laughing, enjoying a meal and celebrating our friendship in my home is truly warming.

Thanks and Giving
Two words to Celebrate Living
We Gather and Grace
Our Home Our Space
With food for our Bodies
And
Nutrition for our Souls
All which makes us Grateful
A Thousand Fold

THANKSGIVING AT FARMDALE
THREE IN THE AFTERNOON

Thanksgiving

Thanksgiving

Thanks and *giving*. Two of my favorite words! Combining them creates a single word, holiday and season I truly love. Fall is my favorite season all around, although there are elements of each season that I enjoy individually. It's a special time of year, as, for many families, it encompasses an entire weekend, not just a day.

Thanksgiving for my family is not unlike many holidays traditionally. With a large and proximate family, we gather and give thanks around the table with the traditions and menu associated therein. Since the majority of us still live nearby, Thanksgiving and its meal are not unlike a lovely Sunday family dinner. So, this gives me the excuse to tweak the traditional style and even set a new tradition. A slight change or update feeds my craving for creativity. This bodes true for the tablescape and décor, too.

I love a Thanksgiving lunch that is a touch lighter than an evening meal—for me, a turkey sandwich would be just fine! A good soup, a good seasonal salad and roasted veggies and sides make for a perfect midday meal—leaving room for dessert, of course!

My dining room at Farmdale is sunny and light-filled by two large windows, and two large mirrors reflect that light back into the room. Brick floors and lighter washed paneling create almost a conservatory feel, and the two large fiddle-leaf ficus trees add to the effect. The direction I take for my tabletop is a visually lighter tableau, with handsome and pretty elements all combined with family and found pieces.

For us down in South Central Georgia, the dahlias give their final salute to the season in late November. After using them for seasonal accents, décor or containers, I replant them in a cutting border, where they can grow wild and have long stems for cutting the next season. These become the stems for my centerpiece. Mimi's silver punch bowl is my go-to container, and the unapologetic billowing of dahlias and mums cascade in shades of peach, apricot, fuchsia, yellow and scarlet. Loquat leaves from the garden serve as greenery and mimic the loquats in the pattern in Lee Jofa fabric on my windows.

A bouquet of the last roses of the season—in my favorite shades of coral, peach and apricot—holds court on the Welsh cupboard, with a spray of nandina berries setting the seasonal tone. Bright yellow branches of Japanese maples strike a contrast against the antique jade vases and peachy glaze of the lamps on the sideboard. My mother's family crest sports pomegranates, so I love to have some represented on the table and sideboard. Large etched-glass hurricanes on the antique Chinese demilunes are filled with branches of magenta sassanquas, autumnal hued dogwood and magnolia—all right from the garden and land.

Thanksgiving

One of my favorite color combinations is peach and brown—apricot and tortoiseshell. Seen in the linens, flatware and stemware, this handsome combo is frequently seen throughout my home and designs. Farmdale is actually painted a dark brown, and my side doors are a favorite shade of Benjamin Moore, Coral Spice.

Vintage turkey plates mix with heirloom turkey salt and pepper shakers—the oldest pair I have are displayed on the Welsh cupboard and belonged to my great-great-grandmother. These festive nods are direct representations of the holiday proper, but other than those Toms, the tableau doesn't necessarily read as Thanksgiving—more of an elegant fall dinner. To me, Thanksgiving is a season of heartfelt reflection and mindset. Holidays are bittersweet, often filled with expectation, memories of loved ones lost and how life changes. I find that in this season, I strive to set a table of thanksgiving within my heart and mind—a feast for the soul to sustain, energize and inspire.

Now with nieces and nephews aplenty—a cornucopia of cousins—I find it important to be the host like my grandmother taught me to be—confident, inclusive, loving and warm. Yes, it means setting a beautiful table, but more importantly, feeding these folks body and soul from my table. I am so grateful for Mimi and Granddaddy and their legacy of love, faith and family bestowed upon me, my sisters and cousins. I might even offer a quiet "thanks for giving" to them. Thanks for giving me so much for which to be truly grateful. As I set the table and see Mimi's punch bowl reflecting the flowers and place settings, and I can't help but think about the dinners and meals and holidays previously reflected. They are all with me today, still. That is Thanksgiving to me!

PRECEDING OVERLEAF: Gathering and giving thanks, in turn—Thanksgiving. I have an affinity for the colors of fall, but often they become heavy by the time the holidays arrive. The last of the dahlias and chrysanthemums from Mary Royal's garden prove otherwise. Celery green seeded-glass goblets mix with tortoiseshell stemware and flatware as a handsome contrast to the pinks, plums and soft oranges of the flowers.

OPPOSITE: Pattern play and repetition are seen in the Chippendale bannister and the dining chairbacks. Branches from the woods and garden in large hurricanes make for easy, dramatic arrangements to flank the living room opening. Truly, it only takes a branch or two to create a wondrous, seasonal display. My family's crest displays pomegranates, so I like to nod to our Granade heritage at our gatherings. Besides, they're absolutely beautiful this time of year.

The dining room windows at Farmdale face south, washing the room in great light that the fiddle-leaf ficus trees love. The light changes throughout the day and seasons, causing the grass cloth on the walls to glow from buttery yellow to peachy hues. My home was designed and built in an intentional, old-fashioned way to tell a story as older homes do. The dining room, née porch, could have been glassed in . . . or some other story. The brick floors, exposed rafters and lofty ceiling give a sense of place.

Thanksgiving

OPPOSITE: My most treasured ironstone piece is the platter in the cupboard, given to Mimi and Granddaddy when they were married in 1955. I asked Mimi about it one time, and she said, "It was old then, given to me by an old lady at our church. She said it was old when she received it." Ha! The turkey salt and pepper shakers were Mimi's grandmother Sarah Ann's, for whom she was named—and we have Sarahs and Anns in the family with each generation.

ABOVE: I have a fondness for white ironstone pieces—tureens, platters and cachepots that are perfect for setting off, displaying and serving. Fall is a fabulous time for roses in the Deep South, and Mary Royal's are stunning; she knows my favorite colors. These glorious stems are a picture of the season, with nandina berries starting to blush with holiday color.

OVERLEAF LEFT: The Japanese maples in the garden turn the most vibrant yellow right around Thanksgiving. I love their contrast with the emerald-hued vases. The painted pheasants are from my dear friends Kayla and George Bruner, who know I love midcentury painted birds.

OVERLEAF RIGHT: Two large mirrors, same scale as the windows opposite, reflect the room and the rafters and hip of the roofline turning the corner. Sassanqua, magnolia and dogwood branches are right from the land and garden.

PAGES 216–17: Punch bowls and pomegranates celebrate the season. Loquat leaves, pompom chrysanthemums, dahlias and cascades of nandina berries and foliage fill Mimi's punch bowl. Majolica bowls from Provvista, my Aunt Kathy Brantley's company, are some of my favorite serving and display pieces. Like mother like daughter, Aunt Kathy serves our family like her mama, my mimi.

PRECEDING OVERLEAF: The view from the living room into the dining room. Fireside is where we find ourselves after the Thanksgiving meal. The painting on the right is of the Leroy Post Office, Washington County, Alabama. My cousin Julia Harwell Segar painted it for my grandfather, Napp, her uncle. This post office was the inspiration for Farmdale. I had seen the painting in Granddaddy's office for as long as I can recall, and he gifted me the painting as a housewarming present when I moved into Farmdale.

OPPOSITE: The last of the hydrangeas and the first of the red berries make a seasonal display for the faux bamboo cupboard. I allow hydrangeas to dry on the bush, and then cut and arrange them. They do the work; there's no need for any tricks or gimmicks.

ABOVE: More of the prettiest roses in all my favorite colors. Peach, coral, apricot and salmon hues are complementary contrasts with the green jardiniere and apples. Schumacher "Le Faisan Chinoiserie" is the inspiration fabric for my living room, as seen in the pillow with the bird.

Thanksgiving

PRECEDING OVERLEAF: More of the season's dried hydrangeas; these are from Joe Pye cottage. The perfect mountain air dries the paniculata species perfectly in September. I may be one of the only people who hauls hydrangeas from one home to another, but it makes me happy! The watercolor on the mantel was painted by Eliza Price after my grandparents' wedding portrait.

OPPOSITE: The Mark Hearld "Squirrel and Sunflower" paper in my pantry is a cheery backdrop for serving pieces, artwork by nieces and nephews, and significant sentimentalities. I spend a good bit of time in the pantry—it's my favorite room at Farmdale just being surrounded by the memories, having coffee and quiet time, or planning my next menu or arranging flowers. It's my Farmer's Pantry, as there is no resident butler.

ABOVE: A still life in the pantry. Local artist Christy Flores painted Farmdale on a platter for me, a gift from my friend Megan Brent at the Perfect Pear downtown. A Charlie West rooster greets the morning, where oranges await squeezing and coffee awaits brewing.

Thanksgiving

OPPOSITE: There are a million turkey recipes and techniques. My friend Sara Jo brines the bird in buttermilk and spatchcocks it. Salt and pepper and that's it! I told her that I'll set the table if she'll bake the bird!

ABOVE: Southerners have "dressing" usually at their Thanksgiving tables, while "stuffing" is more common outside the South. Sara Jo took an interpretation of the two and made a stuffing with cornbread and croissants. "After all, you are from Perry!" she said with a French flair. My great-great-grandmother Sarah Ann's turkey plates still grace our table. Only a few remain, but they are special indeed. My friend Vicky Griffin found some other lovely turkey plates for me after I had broken some of Sarah Ann's one Thanksgiving. Vicky said, "No one will ever know these were not hers!"

Thanksgiving

ABOVE: Sampson and I stand amidst potted pansies and violas in citrus shades of lemon, orange and tangerine. I love to host a mid-afternoon meal, allowing the evening to be leftovers and more relaxed.

OPPOSITE: Often the Thanksgiving menu becomes a cornucopia of casseroles. A few twists on tradition include hasselback butternut squash, roasted carrots and parsnips with thyme and parsley, a sweet potato soup that is perfect anytime this season, a pumpkin poundcake, Fuji apple green salad and cranberry relish. This works great for Thanksgiving or any fall meal.

Thanksgiving

You're Invited to Gather at
Farmdale
For Christmas Celebrations
Eleven in the morning

'Tis the Season of Comfort and Joy
Rejoice! Rejoice!
Emmanuel, God is with us

Comfort & Joy

Comfort & Joy

"... Tidings of comfort and joy—*comfort* and *joy*!" These two words are repeated and reinforced to us in the Christmas tune "God Rest Ye Merry Gentleman." In fact, I find it humorous that it takes the Almighty to "rest" us this season! It's a busy time, for sure!

Christmas brings a sleighful of emotions with its advent. I often enter the season with some heaviness in my heart. Having lost my mother and grandparents, I carry the grief for them along with the memories of Christmases past. Yet, it is the restoration of comfort and joy that I strive to set as the season begins. I find that the comfort of friendship, the joy of the new generations in our family and the merriment these create sustains me far longer than tinsel and trees. Amidst the hurried schedules of programs and parties, family events and festivities, I long for the comfort of home and the joy of the season to be evident in my spirit—which, in all honesty, is probably more difficult than hanging the garland up the stairwell.

One of my dearest friends from Auburn and still to this day is Mary Cox Brown, of Marigold Designs. She has brought comfort and joy to me since our college days and brings and laughter and fun still! She and her team of Marigold mavens have helped to restore the glad tidings of this season when I need it. Mary Cox understands how I crave the comforts of seasons past, the joy of seasons present, and especially how I love to use the heirlooms of my mother and grandmother with jaunty additions of today.

"Silver and Gold," "The Holly and the Ivy" . . . "Deck the Halls" . . . "O Christmas Tree" . . . so many lyrics and words are apropos to holiday decorating! Mary Cox and her team truly decked the halls of Farmdale and anything else that stood still! I love to use fresh foliage from the garden and woods, amaryllis and ilex berries, potted paperwhites and pine cones galore—all accented with colorful ribbons and woven wreaths celebrating the season. It's amazing how a friend can not only know your heart but know what your heart needs—and Mary Cox truly does.

"Remind me the story of your mama's Christmas china," Mary Cox inquired—knowing that was a great way for me to reminisce and remind me of my mama as we set the table. As the story goes, Mama went into labor with me in an antique shop while buying Christmas china—the very set shown here! I was a June baby, so a very pregnant mother-to-be buying Christmas china in June was the least of the store owner's concerns that day. He had to call my father and inform him what hospital to go to—and to pay the bill for the china! "Only you would decide to be born in an antique shop!" Mary Cox said. We laughed and laughed as if we'd never heard that story before—and to be honest, it gets better and better with each telling!

Comfort & Joy

My dining room serves double duty as entry hall, so guests are greeted with a set table or buffet upon entering Farmdale. Filling Mimi's silver punch bowl with amaryllis and magnolia, Mary Cox and I created "satellites" to "orbit" around the centerpiece from a mix of Mama's glass and crystal bowls filled with peonies, roses and ranunculus. Red and green truly reign supreme at Christmas, but mine and Mama's favorite color—coral, or "carl" as she said it—mixes fabulously with said holiday duo. A George Spencer check fabric was tailored as a tablecloth and sets off the flowers and place settings with a festive flair.

Mixing red with coral is dramatic and fresh—and offsetting these colors with complementary blue and white jardinieres or pottery is traditional yet fresh. It's the homage to traditional styles that provides some comfort and the twists on the traditions that sparks joy! With a spectrum of color from persimmon to chartreuse, red and green fit right in the middle comfortably, and the colorful family of tones, hues and tints makes things merry and bright. However, magnolia and holly take precedence as my favorite foliage, and adding cut stems of amaryllis, pine cones or ribbons adds a further nod to the season. The brown magnolia is the perfect cinnamon hue, echoing the pine cones and a perfect complement to other foliage and flowers.

Wreaths are not limited to doors and windows alone; chairbacks, mirrors and shelves can host a wreath or two! The lovely red satin Shuler Studio wreath sashes are set off by blue juniper wreaths on the inside of my dining room doors—a favorite place to unexpectedly hang a wreath.

PRECEDING OVERLEAF: "If it sits still, I'll put a wreath on it. I take that back, I have a wreath on my car," my dear friend Mary Cox Brown said. She and her team at Marigold Designs in Birmingham helped me transform Farmdale into a Christmas wonderland. Wreaths on the backs of the dining chairs was a favorite touch. Made of rosemary, they delightfully scented the room.

OPPOSITE: My mother's Christmas china, which she bought in a shop and then went into labor with me, is my treasured place setting for the season. Mimi's silver, glasses and napkins include her in the Christmas tableau. Bowls of amaryllis, roses, peonies and ranunculus dot the table.

Comfort & Joy

OPPOSITE: My sideboard in its Christmas splendor. Foxtail lilies, amaryllis and ilex berries sprout from green vases. I keep pomegranates on the sideboard as a familial gesture to our crest, dressed up with a bit of holly and ivy in a nod to one of my favorite Christmas songs.

ABOVE: My pine dresser is dotted with peachy glazed vases filled with flowers. Mary Cox gave the dresser magnolia pine cone "pigtails," as she called the garland above. The large sugar cones and brown-back magnolia leaves are such a handsome complement to the pretty flowers and china.

Comfort & Joy

I have an adage I like to adhere to for decorating: "You have to score three 'Fs' to make an 'A plus.'" Fruit, flowers and foliage—this trio bodes well throughout the year and always scores an A plus in my grade book! Whether jewel-toned citrus, bright green apples or ruby red pomegranates, arranging a basket, bowl or platter of fruit is an easy trick of the trade for lovely décor, especially when offset by the foliage and flowers of the season. I have always loved the Williamsburg style of combining fruit, flowers and foliage and carry this theme from the outdoor designs to the interior schemes as well.

I love to host either a brunch or mid-afternoon lunch for Christmas—but, really, it's a day of grazing. My sisters and I usually have breakfast or brunch together, and the family at large joins for lunch or "lupper"—a meal between lunch and supper. My dear friend Sara Jo McLean helps me with catering and cooking for the whole herd. From the goodies reminiscent of our childhood to the delightful new dishes at our table, she always helps me keep my "flocks by night" fed. Whether a coconut cake filled with fresh cranberry relish between the layers, the roast and potatoes, or mascarpone with ginger cookies, we surely celebrate with food in this family!

Fresh fruit, flowers and foliage may not last as long as artificial alternatives, and for me that works just fine. It is their symbolism and short season that reminds me of life, to celebrate the moment and live it joyfully. The lyric from the hymn "Hail to the Lord's Anointed" comes to mind: "He shall come down like showers upon the fruitful earth; love, joy, and hope, like flowers, spring in His path to birth."

As with Thanksgiving, the truer meaning of this holiday is what I treasure most. Merriest of times amidst grief makes for a complementary spirit in the season. Being merry at Christmas is about sending out comfort and joy to the world—and I hope that truly makes heaven and nature sing!

Mama, Mimi and myself are all represented in some fashion on the table. The George Spencer Designs check fabric is the merriest green to offset the reds, pinks, peaches and whites of the tablescape. Whenever I hear someone say they cannot find the right size tablecloth, I like to remind them they can always have one made. Simple tailoring, from our clothes to tablecloths, makes all the difference.

Comfort & Joy

Comfort & Joy

ABOVE: Wreaths and arrangements flank the living room entry on antique Chinese demilunes. The pair of hurricanes filled with branches and blossoms each season or event are an ode to the niches in the Great Hall filled with fabulous flowers at the Metropolitan Museum of Art in New York, where, thanks to an endowment, the niches are forever in flower, created by the master floral designer Remco van Vliet. They always inspire me when I visit the city.

OPPOSITE: Velvety textured and cinnamon-hued backs of magnolia leaves set off the flowers and fruits of the season: amaryllis in salmon and red, Burford holly berries and arching stems of leucothoe.

OVERLEAF LEFT: We refer to stacked platters and paintings as "snowmen." They are the only snowmen we get to create in Perry! A "snowman" of favored, treasured platters creates a central column in the displayed collection of my pine cupboard.

OVERLEAF RIGHT: One of the easiest and most elegant holiday displays, to me, is citrus and red berries. They last so long too! Scrumptious cheese biscuits await gobbling up next to the berries and oranges.

Comfort & Joy

PRECEDING OVERLEAF: "A choir of amaryllis" is what floral designer Mary Cox dubbed my mantel. "Glory in the highest, indeed!" I replied. Mama's amaryllis screen is like a reflection of the mantel above. Blue spruce, magnolia and ilex berries keep a festive touch, and the peachy pink velvet ribbons suspend the wreaths, carrying the color from the dining room and mantel throughout.

OPPOSITE: Red amaryllis, a collar of pepper berries and magnolia burst forth from my blue and white jar. I truly love the traditional red and green color scheme, but adding pops of coral, pink and shades therein add pizzazz.

ABOVE: When the halls are decked, the mantel decorated and the table set, I feel the Christmas tree doesn't have to be the grandest of them all. A smaller tree in a foot bowl serves as my tree on a table skirted in a Claremont pattern. The stairwell is girded with a garland of sapphire juniper up the banister and accented with spectacular sugar pine cones hung with coral and green velvet ribbons.

Comfort & Joy

PRECEDING OVERLEAF: Cards and photos are displayed on the fridges, wreaths of bay leaves are hung on the shelves and window, and seasonal fruit and foliage decorate the island. The rendering of Farmdale is by my nephew, Napp Yelton.

OPPOSITE: My kitchen table is decked in green and white, which is always right! I found the large brass deer at an antique show and named her Merry Vixon. My family has a history of naming objects, from cars to, well, large brass deer. A snowman of rosemary leaves bejeweled with lemons and soft blue ribbon anchors the kitchen window.

ABOVE: A bay leaf wreath is hung in the bay window—how apropos! The light from this box bayed window is perfect for growing myrtle topiaries. Some of the most elegant holiday displays can be composed of fruit!

OVERLEAF LEFT AND RIGHT: Coconut cake is a holiday staple in Southern tradition. My friend Sara Jo helped me tweak the recipes in *A Time to Cook* and *A Time to Celebrate*, adding a fresh cranberry layer. The tart brightness of the cranberries complements the sweetness of the coconut. A spice tea is served through the holidays at Farmdale. In Nashville, Tennessee, it's served at the Picnic Cafe and is called Picnic Punch. I love it over ice or warm.

Comfort & Joy

PRECEDING OVERLEAF LEFT: A forest of topiaries with jaunty yellow ribbons are collected on the back hallway table and last until the new year with the light from the large windows. The vintage rope lamps inspired the yellow ribbons. The artwork above is by my college friend and accomplished artist Emily York Ozier "EMYO."

PRECEDING OVERLEAF RIGHT: The back door boasts a wreath made of variegated Algerian ivy leaves. The red sash and coral door are reminiscent of the Christmas colors inside.

OPPOSITE: Boxwood wreaths are displayed on the Waller Room windows. The "Treasure Flower" pattern by Cowtan and Tout dresses the windows and inspired the blue-and-green theme of the wreaths and ribbons. Amaryllis, pepperberry, Star of Bethlehem and roses make for lovely holiday bouquets. My friend and fellow Auburn grad Erika Powell's fabric is seen on the pillows.

ABOVE: A grouping of some favorite things for the season: forced paperwhites, amaryllis and Christmas candy. The Charlie West lamps add warmth to the color scheme of the room. The wicker-wrapped jars are go-to containers for vases, hurricanes or display.

PRECEDING OVERLEAF LEFT: The garden gate and pigeonniers are decked in holiday finery. I am always inspired by Colonial Williamsburg and take that approach to holiday décor outside at Farmdale.

PRECEDING OVERLEAF RIGHT: I love to give potted plants as Christmas gifts. From topiaries to forced bulbs like paperwhites and amaryllis, flowers and foliage make for cheery gifts and are fun for a gardener to pot together too.

RIGHT: Ilex and magnolia fill my garden gate entry urns for the holidays. Ann Kelly, a dear friend in Albany, Georgia, makes the most gorgeous wreaths of pine, magnolia and juniper. They are the perfect gestures to welcome the season, friends and family to Farmdale.

OPPOSITE: A garland of evergreens, citrus and ilex is swagged across the door. Aren't the brown backs of magnolia leaves a fabulous color?

ABOVE: A welcoming badge of pineapple, privet berry, citrus, holly and magnolia anchors the front railing at Farmdale. Lush, citrine velvet ribbons contrast with the glossy green magnolia wreaths on the doors and windows.

OVERLEAF LEFT: Up the steps, a magnolia garland guides the way. Baskets of vibrant red ilex berries are spectacular specimens to use in the garden and home through the Christmas season. Antique urns with years of patina flank the front door like bubbling fountains filled with pine cones, greens and berries.

OVERLEAF RIGHT: My syrup kettle fountain greets friends and family at the front entry of Farmdale. A magnolia garland is hung with the handsome contrast of brown and green leaves. Traditional Fraser Fir wreaths anchor the larger windows.

Acknowledgments

It takes a village. From child raising to writing a book, and I have the best village!

Margaret Sullivan Keyes—thank you! Your constant joy and delightfully lovely spirit are good and perfect gifts in my life and to so many others. Thank you, too, to your mother, Jane Anne, who taught you how to celebrate beautifully and thoughtfully, as her mother taught her. Jane Anne, I love and thank you for all you do for us!

Thank you to my James Farmer Incorporated staff and design team. Y'all inspire me and continue to seek and create beauty with me for our homes and our clients. Jesse, Haley, Melanie, Ellen, Ashley, Corie and Lizzie—y'all are an amazing team that allows me to dream and accomplish goals every year. Thank you, ladies!

Acknowledgments

To my family—y'all gave me the traditions I continue today. Bee and Papa, my sisters, my cousins, my nieces and nephews, y'all are the limbs and branches of the roots from which we've grown! Aunt Sally, you're our loving link to our grandparents and Uncle K; thank you for being the best friend to Mimi and aunt to us all! Mimi, Granddaddy and Mama gave us the ability to tap into their rich soil of love, and because of that legacy, we are able to truly flourish and celebrate!

Will—thank you for loving me and putting up with me! You've brought so much laughter, love and joy to my life, and I look forward to celebrating more and more with you.

Emily Followill—what can I say! It's never work; it's always a true joy! Thank you for capturing our creations with the artistic eye only you can! Your friendship over the years is a bonus on top of your incredible photography! Thanks so much for everything!

Karen Hirons and Drew English—y'all are the ones who should be writing this book! Thank you, my friends, for all you did for this book and for me each and every day! I am so excited to celebrate in the mountains with y'all every season.

To my flower power team—Mary Royal, Mary Pinson, Libby Endry, Sandy Linebaugh—you ladies grow, arrange and provide the most gorgeous flowers that make my life and the lives of those around you more beautiful with your floral prowess and graciousness. Thank you for the flowers seen throughout this book and for everything.

Mary Cox Brown and the Marigold mavens—y'all made Christmas a dream come true at Farmdale. Mary Cox, your friendship from Auburn and today is a true treasure! Thank you for being a fabulous friend!

Susie—you keep the home fires going! Thank you! My home is warm and welcoming thanks to your skills and hospitality. We have so many fun times ahead and many wonderful memories too! Thanks for all you do for me and my family.

Sara Jo—chef, counselor, food stylist and friend—thank you! You and Vicki are truly amazing at what you do! You make delicious food, create inviting dishes and menus and tell me when I've planned too much! Thank you for all the goodies and yummy food, not only in these pages, but for all the years beforehand and to come.

Emmie Ruth Wise, Mary Carpenter and Eliza Price—your artistry and skill sets inspire me and your talents are astounding! Thank you for always being there for me and taking creative visions and bringing them to life.

Rita Sowins—thank you for your lovely book design and for working with my "suggestions."

Madge Baird—my editor at Gibbs Smith—thank you. Those two little words are intended to cover so much! You've believed in me since the very first book, and now this makes ten! Thank you to the Gibbs Smith team, as well, for supporting you and me and our endeavors. I'm looking forward to the next chapter!

First Edition
26 25 24 23 22   5 4 3 2 1

Text © 2022 James T. Farmer III
Photographs © 2022 Emily Followill, except
© 2022 Meredith Farmer Photography, 4, 270
Illustrations by Emmie Ruth Wise, © 2022 James T. Farmer III

All rights reserved. No part of this book may be reproduced by any means whatsoever without written permission from the publisher, except brief portions quoted for purpose of review.

Published by
Gibbs Smith
P.O. Box 667
Layton, Utah 84041
1.800.835.4993 orders
www.gibbs-smith.com

Designed by Rita Sowins / Sowins Design
Printed and bound in China

Gibbs Smith books are printed on paper produced from sustainable PEFC-certified forest/controlled wood source. Learn more at www.pefc.org.

Library of Congress Control Number: 2021953446
ISBN 978-1-4236-5795-8